# Aboriginal Fishing Rights

# Aboriginal Fishing Rights
## Laws, Courts and Politics

Parnesh Sharma

Fernwood Publishing • Halifax

Editing: Douglas Beall
Cover photo: Circa 1880, Siwash "Indians" curing salmon along the banks of the Fraser River. Vancouver Public Library Archives Photograph number 3257.
Design and production: Beverley Rach
Printed and bound in Canada by: Hignell Printing Limited


A publication of:
Fernwood Publishing
Box 9409, Station A
Halifax, Nova Scotia
B3K 5S3

Fernwood Publishing Company Limited gratefully acknowledges the financial support of the Ministry of Canadian Heritage and the Nova Scotia Department of Education and Culture.




**Canadian Cataloguing in Publication Data**

Sharma, Parnesh.

     Aboriginal fishing rights

     Includes bibliographical references.
     ISBN 1-895686-98-9

1. Indians of North America -- Fishing -- Law and legislation -- British Columbia.
2. Indians of North America -- Canada -- Claims.   3. Indians of North America -- Canada -- Legal status, laws, etc. -- Canada.   I. Title.

KEB529.5.H8S52 1998     346.71104'6956     C98-950006-3

for my mother and father

# Contents

# List of Abbreviations

| | |
|---|---|
| AFN | Assembly of First Nations |
| AFS | Aboriginal Fisheries Strategy |
| BCCA | British Columbia Court of Appeal |
| DFO | Department of Fisheries and Oceans |
| FTA | Free Trade Agreement |
| G7 | Group of Seven |
| NIB | National Indian Brotherhood |
| PSA | Pilot Sales Agreement |
| SCC | Supreme Court of Canada |

## FIRST NATIONS WHOSE STATEMENTS OF INTENT TO NEGOTIATE A TREATY HAVE BEEN ACCEPTED AS OF NOVEMBER 1, 1994 BY THE B.C. TREATY COMMISSION

1. Alkali Nation
2. Tsleil Waututh Nation also known as Burrard Nation
3. Cariboo Tribal Council
4. Carrier Sekani Tribal Council
5. Champagne and Aishihik First Nations
6. Ditidaht First Nation
7. The Gitanyow Hereditary Chiefs
8. Gitksan Nation
9. Council of the Haida Nation
10. Haisla Nation
11. Heiltsuk Nation
12. Homalco Indian Band
13. Hul'qumi'num First Nations
14. In-shuck-ch
15. Kaska Dena Council
16. Katzie Indian Band
17. Klahoose
18. Ktunaxa/Kinbasket Tribal Council
19. Kwakiutl First Nations*
20. Lheit-lit'en Nation
21. Musqueam Nation
22. Nanaimo Nation
23. Nat'oot'en Nation*
24. Nuu Chah Nulth Tribal Council
25. Nazko Indian Band*
26. Oweekeno Nation
27. Pavilion*
28. Sechelt Indian Band
29. Sliammon Indian Band
30. Squamish Nation
31. Spallumcheen Indian Band*
32. Taku River Tlingit First Nation
33. Te'mexw Treaty Association*
34. Teslin Tlingit Council*
35. Treaty 8 Tribal Association
36. Tsawwassen* First Nation
37. Tsay Keh Dene Band
38. Tsimshian Nation
39. Westbank
40. Wet'suwet'en Nation
41. Xaxli'p People
42. Yale First Nation

* Maps of traditional territories of these First Nations are not available at this time: Kwakiutl First Nation, Nat'oot'en Nation, Nazko Indian Band, Pavillion, Spallumcheen Indian Band, Te'mexw Treaty Association (Association comprised of Douglas Treaty Bands), Tsawwassen First Nation and the Teslin Tlingit Council.

The information shown on this map does not imply that the First Nations and the Governments of Canada and British Columbia have agreed to the boundaries.

For information on the B.C. Treaty Commission Process Please call 1-800-665-8330 or (604) 775-2078.

# TRADITIONAL TERRITORIES OF BRITISH COLUMBIA FIRST NATIONS

# Acknowledgements

There are many persons I wish to thank, for without their assistance this book would not have been completed.

First and foremost, a most sincere thanks to Chief Joe Becker of the Musqueam Indian Band. Chief Becker gave freely of his time and patiently explained to me the nuances of aboriginal fishing rights. Mr. Becker reviewed the contents of portions of this book for accuracy and provided insightful information, taking time from his busy schedule to meet with or speak to me on the telephone; for that I am most grateful. I would also like to thank members of the Musqueam Indian Band for sharing their experiences with me.

An equally profound thanks to Terry Glavin, author, fisher and former "native beat" reporter; Mr. Glavin provided valuable insight, often pointing me in helpful directions and providing important contacts (who, after learning I had been referred by Mr. Glavin, also spoke to me at length and assisted me in my research). Mr. Glavin also reviewed draft copies of this manuscript and provided constructive feedback. He put up with my countless phone calls at all hours and was always willing to help out. Sincere thanks also to William Duncan, senior administrative officer, Department of Fisheries and Oceans (DFO). Mr. Duncan was most helpful and provided the department's perspective on central issues. A big thanks to a senior manager at the DFO, who quite understandably wishes to remain anonymous. I am also grateful to David Ellis, fisher, author and now fisheries consultant, for his advice and understanding. Mr. Ellis provided valuable information, referred me to other contacts and was always available to discuss the issues with me. I would also like to thank the Native International Trade Association for allowing me to attend their conference for a fraction of what other participants paid, and for providing me with copies of papers presented at the conference.

Even though I was often critical of their positions, I would like to thank Michael Hunter, president of the Fisheries Council of British Columbia and Phil Eidsvik, spokesperson for the British Columbia Fisheries Survival Coalition, for their time and for providing a different perspective on fishing. I am also thankful to Mel Smith for sending me a copy of his article on aboriginal fishing rights.

A sincere thanks also to key interviewees: Marvin Storrow of Blake, Cassels and Graydon, Vancouver, B.C., counsel for Ron Sparrow; Maria Morellato of Blake, Cassels and Graydon, Vancouver, B.C., counsel; Judge Cunliffe Barnet, Williams Lake, B.C.; and Parcival Copes, Fisheries Institute,

Simon Fraser University.

I also wish to thank Professor Bob Ratner, Department of Anthropology and Sociology, University of British Columbia, for his advice and feedback on draft copies, and for his patience and understanding. I would also like to thank Professor Tissa Fernando and Chief Steven Point, lawyer and aboriginal rights activist, for providing constructive comment.

Others contributed their opinions and insights, and to all of them I am most grateful. The responsibility for this work and any shortcomings it may contain are mine.

# Preface

Aboriginal rights, and aboriginal fishing rights in particular, are topics that elicit a variety of responses, ranging from positive to hostile. In British Columbia, fish is big business and the fourth largest industry. The stakes are high and the positions of the various user groups and stakeholders are clearly set out. The fight over fish has pitted aboriginal groups against other aboriginal groups, as well as against the federal government and its department of fisheries and oceans. However, the fight becomes vicious, underhanded and mean spirited when the aboriginal groups face off against the commercial industry.

In an attempt to even the odds, the aboriginal peoples have turned to the courts for recognition and protection of what they view as an inherent right, that is, the right to fish, which arose out of the very nature of being an aboriginal person. Until the Supreme Court of Canada decision in *R. v. Sparrow,* aboriginal rights had been virtually ignored by both the courts and the state. However, *Sparrow* changed all that and significantly altered the fight over fish. And that fight has become a virtually no-holds-barred battle.

The *Sparrow* decision remains to this day one of the most important Supreme Court decisions related to aboriginal rights. This book is a case study of *Sparrow.* It examines the decision as well as the ability of subordinate or disadvantaged groups to use the law to advance their causes for social progress and equality.

I also examine the status and nature of aboriginal fishing rights before and after the *Sparrow* decision. And I discuss whether the principles of the decision have been upheld by the courts or followed by the government of Canada. My findings are based on interviews with representatives of the key players in the fishing industry, namely, the Musqueam Indian Band, the Department of Fisheries and Oceans (DFO) and the commercial industry.

What I have found does not bode well for the aboriginal peoples—the principles of the *Sparrow* decision have not been followed by the government of Canada, and aboriginal fishing rights remain subject to arbitrary control. This book examines why and how this has happened.

# Chapter One

# Introduction

The fight over fish is nothing new. It dates back at least to the beginning of the arrival of white settlers in Canada. Even then the battle lines were clearly drawn—it was the interests of the white commercial industry versus the interests of the aboriginal peoples. An article in the *Vancouver Province,* dated November 19, 1904, reveals the tone:

> INDIANS WIPING OUT SOCKEYE
> A report in detail concerning the manner in which Indians at the headwaters of the Skeena and other northern rivers are striking at the very root of the life of the salmon-fishing industry in British Columbia, one of the greatest sources of the people's wealth, has been received .
> . . no less than 2,000,000 salmon . . . were killed in the Indian traps this year. That number of fish, if canned, would make about 142,857 cases (in Newell 1993: 91).

The fight over fish, of which (sockeye) salmon is commercially the most valuable, has all the makings of a classic showdown. The cast of players includes the aboriginal peoples of Canada, the commercial fishing industry and the government of Canada; also jockeying for positions are numerous interest groups, labour unions and provincial governments. The subject of fishing, particularly aboriginal fishing rights, is a highly emotional and controversial issue. The very existence of coastal communities, the wealth of powerful corporations, the hopes of an impoverished minority and the employment prospects of thousands of workers rest mightily upon the denizens of the deep. The fish, oblivious to their importance, are an imperiled species and may in the very near future cease to exist, having been fished to extinction by a variety of user groups who share at best an acrimonious relationship fuelled by greed, ignorance and racism.

Access to fish is jealously guarded and fought over on various fronts. The fight is underhanded, vicious and mean-spirited, and in recent times, particularly since the Supreme Court of Canada decision in *R.* v. *Sparrow,* the courts have entered the fray. The *Sparrow* decision remains the most important and controversial decision on aboriginal fishing rights and was the first decision to apply the provisions of section 35(1) in the aboriginal rights section of the *Constitution Act, 1982.*

## MINORITY RIGHTS, THE LAW,
## EQUALITY AND SOCIAL TRANSFORMATION

In September 1982, with much fanfare and great expectations, the Canadian *Charter of Rights and Freedoms* was proclaimed. This proclamation had been preceded by intense debate, not only regarding the repatriation of the Canadian Constitution but, more importantly, the inclusion of a charter of rights and freedoms. On the latter issue, over twelve hundred groups and individuals made representations to the Special Joint Committee on the Canadian Constitution (Mahoney 1992: 228). Three years later, when section 15, or the equality clause, of the *Charter*, became effective, scenes of minority-group celebrations flashed across the nation's television screens. These groups were anticipating a renewal and strengthening of their rights and freedoms, which were now guaranteed by the *Charter*. The celebrations were based on the hope and perception that the *Charter* would provide empowerment, not only to combat discrimination and challenge the status quo, but to achieve a real measure of equality that had so far eluded the have-nots and the powerless of Canadian society.

The proclamation of the *Charter* brought to the forefront a still-continuing argument on the transformative capacity of law. Much has been debated about the capacity of the law to transform existing relations of domination and subordination. According to Sargent (1991: 1), "the role of the law as an arena for social and political change has increasingly climbed to the top of the intellectual calendar for many sociologists of law and legal theorists alike." As evidenced by numerous challenges before the courts (see Mandel 1989; Fine 1992), the hope that the law, or at least the law as it is interpreted and applied by the courts, will ameliorate one's lot in life and remove barriers to equality has been embraced by diverse groups such as as the women's movement to environmental coalitions and aboriginal peoples.

According to law professor Judy Fudge (1990: 47), the perception or belief that litigating constitutionally entrenched legal rights encourages social transformation appears to be based almost entirely on theoretical considerations rather than substantive evidence; that is, most arguments on the transformative capacity of the law assume that winning court cases automatically translates into rights. However, social transformation is not that simple. For example, even though laws regulating access to abortion services were declared unconstitutional (*R.* v. *Morgentaler*) in 1988, access to abortion services remains problematic for the subordinate and powerless groups in society because some provincial governments have refused to fund abortion services or abortion clinics. While the wealthy of Canadian society are able to obtain such services at private clinics or through private doctors, the underprivileged have limited choices and are often dependent upon government-funded clinics for medical services. Even though women's groups celebrated the "abortion victory" as a formal recognition of women's rights, little attention was paid to the remaining, and newly erected, structural barriers. The government of Newfoundland agreed to fund abortion services only some five years after the historic Supreme Court decision in *Morgentaler*, and only after consistently losing court challenges over its refusal to do so.

## THE *Constitution Act, 1982* AND ABORIGINAL RIGHTS

This book focuses on the use of law for social progress. Specifically, I will ask whether section 35(1) of the *Constitution Act, 1982*, lived up to its promise of protecting aboriginal rights. What are the possibilities and limitations of using law in the struggle for social transformation? Does a legal recognition of rights lead to social progress? If so, is it an effective strategy to pursue this recognition? To better understand the larger question of law and social transformation, I will examine one aspect of the debate: how the aboriginal peoples of Canada have used the courts to further their fight for access to a valuable resource—fish. To address this issue, I will examine the landmark and historic Supreme Court of Canada decision on aboriginal rights in the case of *R. v. Sparrow*. I will examine the effectiveness of using law for social transformation by analyzing legal rights before and after *Sparrow,* with particular focus on the legal rights regarding access to fish.

Fish is of vital and fundamental importance to some aboriginal peoples living near the ocean or bodies of freshwater, and it plays a significant role in religious and ceremonial activities. Fish is also viewed as an economic saviour, a means by which many aboriginal bands and tribes hope to create sustainable economic activity. This study will detail the fight over fish and provide an examination of the events leading to the *Sparrow* decision, the decision itself and the events after the decision. Finally I will examine the impact *Sparrow* has had on aboriginal fishing rights and access to fish.

## WHAT IS SOCIAL TRANSFORMATION AND WHY LEGAL RIGHTS?

The measurement of social transformation is not easily reducible, and improvements for the disadvantaged cannot be easily attributed to a single cause. The factors that lead to social transformation occur over time and are varied and complex. However for ease of analysis, I will adapt Snider's (in Brickey and Comack 1986: 169) definition of "reform" to what I mean by social transformation: "[a] change leading to the improvement in the life chances of the disadvantaged versus the advantaged."

Legal victories do not necessarily translate into removals of barriers, structural or otherwise. However, they do provide a measure of success when institutions that appear to serve the ruling classes recognize and concede the "rightness" of arguments presented by subordinate groups. Such decisions have significant impact on how governments (or the ruling classes) deal or relate with subordinate groups. According to McCormick (1993: 523),

The rewards of victory are not necessarily limited to success in the immediate case, but can also involve favourable interpretations of statutes or legal principles, or favourable variations in rules for the applications of those principles, that will govern the resolution of similar controversies in the future.

For example, the Native Affairs minister of Ontario (citing *Sparrow*) stated that "recent court decisions are not only upholding Indian (fishing) rights, but are sending a clear message that governments should begin negotiating with natives" (in Platiel 1993: A7).

According to Fudge (1992: 153), "[R]ights litigation [has] the potential to mobilize social movements, influence the general terms of political debate, change a particular law or doctrine and introduce a variety of perspectives and experiences into the courts which have historically been excluded." To critics who would dismiss such a premise, the question that begs to be asked is, what other feasible options are there. One cannot ignore the political, legal, economic and practical realities of modern nation-states, and the inherent virtues and vices that form part of the package. Notwithstanding academic theorizing and short of an outright revolution, reality necessitates that one work within the parameters, defined by the state, to change society. The apparent paradox that one must play by society's rules to change that society is reconciled by the very nature of law. According to E.P. Thompson (1977: 263),

> the essential precondition for the effectiveness of law . . . is that it shall display an independence from gross manipulation and shall seem to be just. It cannot be seen to do so without upholding its own logic and criteria of equity; indeed on occasion, by actually being just.

## WHY ABORIGINAL PEOPLES OF CANADA?

The focus on aboriginal peoples of Canada is no accident. By almost any measure—social, economic or political—aboriginal peoples are the most powerless and subordinate group in Canadian society. Prior to the *Constitution Act, 1982*, aboriginal peoples had no legal rights unless specifically provided for in legislation and, even then, aboriginal rights were virtually ignored by the Canadian courts—one court simply declared that aboriginal rights were too vague to recognize (Elliott 1991: 25; Sanders 1990: 125). The aboriginal peoples are the "David" and the Canadian state the "Goliath," and more often than not they have fought their battles in various courthouses across Canada. And particularly in the wake of the *Constitution Act, 1982*, and *Sparrow,* the aboriginal peoples have turned to the courts more and more.

Aboriginal peoples make up 14 percent of the population of Saskatchewan, yet they represent 64 percent of the prison population. Nationally the figures are 2 percent and 10 percent respectively (Makin 1987). In a society of unequals, aboriginal peoples are the least equal. A cursory glance at some social indices paints a dismal picture: the life span of an aboriginal person is ten years less than the national average. For status Indians, those registered under the *Indian Act*, the situation is even worse. Life expectancy among this group is twenty years below the national average. In 1974 the infant mortality rate for status Indians was 3.9 per one thousand, and for the Inuit, it was 6.4, compared to the national average of 1.5. A status Indian infant is three times as likely to die a violent or accidental death than other Canadian children; between 35 percent and 75 percent of aboriginal peoples are chronically unemployed; violent death and suicide is a staggering three times the national average—the suicide rate of Canadian aboriginal youth is the highest in the western world. Many aboriginal peoples, particularly status Indians, live on remote reserves in third world-like conditions. Most reserves lack basic necessities, such as indoor plumbing and heating, electricity and access to educational and medical services (Wright 1992a; Valentine 1980: 81–90; Havemann 1989: 56; *Globe and Mail,* April 4, 1990: A6). Recently the *Report of the Aboriginal Justice Inquiry of Manitoba* concluded, "Canada's treatment of its first citizens has been an international disgrace" (in Roberts and York 1991: A1).

Aboriginal peoples of Canada are not homogenous but have a diversity of cultures, circumstances and histories. However, for the purpose of analysis, here the term *aboriginal peoples* refers to all persons who are legally recognized as aboriginal—such as Metis, Inuit, and status and treaty Indians. This distinction is important because whatever legal rights are "won" accrue only to those who are so legally entitled. Notwithstanding the legal and non-legal differences, aboriginal peoples of Canada share a similar fate, a fate that has rendered a once proud people economically and politically powerless and placed them at the very bottom of the Canadian social and power structure.

## LAW AND SOCIAL CHANGE

The seeming omnipotence of law shrouds the concept in mystique. What is law? For some it is a codification of what is right for society, an expression of morality and ideology, of norms and regulations, based on a society-wide consensus. For others, law is an outcome of ongoing or particular conflicts between the powerful and powerless, with the result that law represents the interests and ideology of the powerful. For still others existing on the margins and periphery of an unequal society, the concept of law is meaningless and alien until one is subjected to its controlling influence.

There appears to be little agreement on the definition of law because it depends on one's perspective. For the purpose of this book, Max Weber's definition is particularly apt:

> an order will be called law if it is externally guaranteed by the probability that coercion (physical or psychological), to bring about

conformity or avenge violation, will be applied by a staff of people holding themselves especially ready for that purpose. (1978: 34)

This definition recognizes the pervasiveness and influence of law in society—which demands conformity and prescribes sanctions for violations—and it includes the institutions or agents of law such as the police, courts and correctional institutions, which are used to enforce conformity and punish violations.

Of particular importance here is the function of the courts. As a central and crucial institution of the law, the courts are often portrayed and viewed as the protector of rights or the final arbiter of justice to whom persons who have been wronged may turn for an equitable solution. Whether the courts do in fact provide justice or protect the rights of minorities remains a topic of considerable debate and is of crucial importance to the study at hand. To understand the role of the courts, the concept of ideology is central in any discussion of law.

According to Milovanovic (1988: 13), perhaps the most important function served by law is ideology. Marx and Engels argued that social knowledge (philosophies, ideals and law) is inextricably linked to the material conditions of those who produce such knowledge. In other words, ideology reflects class interests because it is produced by and for class interests, and it is crucial in maintaining and perpetuating the political status quo. The concept of ideology is central to my argument—it is ideology that leads us to believe that all members of society are equal before and under the law. Such ideology obscures the social reality that Canadian society is rife with inequality and contradictions, and not all who appear before the law are equal.

A considerable body of literature examines the relationship between dominant classes and subordinate classes. E.P. Thompson's (1977) analysis of the *Black Act* in eighteenth-century England, and Douglas Hay's *Albion's Fatal Tree* (1975) are classic examples. Unfortunately, few scholars have examined whether law can be used to advance the causes of subordinate groups in any substantive way. Although a body of literature focusing on the transformative capacity of law is emerging, most of it is highly theoretical and lacks concrete supportive evidence. However, the work of Mandel (1989, 1994, 1996) and Brickey and Comack (1986, 1989) merits attention for presenting substantive and contrary arguments regarding the transformative capacity of law.

Law professor Michael Mandel's book *The Charter of Rights and the Legalization of Politics in Canada* (1989) is an incisive analysis of the *Charter*, judicial decision-making and liberal discourse in general. Mandel's Marxist critique is scathing and unrelenting, and leaves no doubt as to his position that law, and the *Charter* in particular, cannot be used for social transformation. According to Mandel (1989: 4):

Where the *Charter* has had an effect, that effect has been to strengthen

18

# Introduction

the already great inequalities in Canada. It has weighed in on the side
of power and, in both crude and subtle ways, has undermined popular
movements . . . [such as] the aboriginal peoples' movement and the
women's movement. Filtering democratic opposition through the
legal system has not only failed to reduce . . . inequalities but has
actually strengthened them.

Mandel's argument that the *Charter* diverts and weakens opposition to the status
quo is evidenced by the subordinate group's reliance on the *Charter* to fight
against inequality. In spite of *Charter* case law, which has overwhelmingly
maintained the status quo, subordinate classes continue to be seduced by the
ideology of the *Charter* and its promise of guaranteed equality.

Mandel's (1989) argument is well worth noting: that the protection and
guarantee of rights enshrined in the *Charter* is often illusory and inconsistent,
and serves to undermine other potentially effective means of seeking redress.
But how does Mandel account for some of the victories won by subordinate
groups? Surely, if one is able to succeed in the courts, then the law has the
potential to become a tool for social reform. Mandel is adamant that law cannot
be used for social reform, and that occasional victories merely uphold the
legitimacy of law.

On the other side of the argument, Brickey and Comack (1986: 321), argue
that

the rhetoric and rules of law must be more than a sham. Law must
provide some protection . . . it must live up to its own claims of equity
and fairness . . . the function of law can differ, depending upon the
relative strength of social forces that struggle around and within the
legal order.

They conclude that it is possible to use law for progressive social changes
because in order for law to maintain the ideology of fairness, it must be seen to
be fair in reality. Brickey and Comack point to examples of rights that are now
constitutionally guaranteed, such as the right to form unions and the right to
strike—rights which were gained by subordinate classes after extensive struggles against the ruling classes.

## The Focus of My Data and Analysis
Is rights litigation an effective way to redress social inequality and have the
courts fulfilled the hopes of the disadvantaged? Disadvantaged groups have
increasingly turned to the courts in their struggles for social equality. Don Ryan,
spokesperson for the Gitksan and Wet'suwet'en peoples, stated that aboriginal
peoples are prepared to wage court battles for eternity in order to get a "fair
shake" from the government (in Simpson 1993: A9).

19

# Aboriginal Fishing Rights

This book will analyze the *Sparrow* decision, undoubtedly the most important Supreme Court of Canada decision to date on aboriginal rights. I will present a critical analysis of the decision, and interviews with officials from the Department of Fisheries and Oceans (DFO) and the members of the Musqueam Indian Band who challenged the state and took the *Sparrow* case to the Supreme Court.

In order to demonstrate the significance of *Sparrow,* I will examine the legal rights to fish before and after the *Sparrow* decision. It is crucial to understand how completely the Canadian courts have denied legal rights to aboriginal peoples. Going back to the words of Chancellor Boyd in the 1886 *St. Catherines Milling* case, Indians were regarded as "heathens and barbarians" with no "fixed abodes," and this had been the position taken by the Supreme Court of Canada, which almost without exception had ruled against aboriginal rights, particularly aboriginal claims to traditional lands and the right to extract resources from those lands.

However, in recent years the Supreme Court of Canada has done an apparent about-face, moving from viewing aboriginal rights with indifference and reluctance to recognizing the aspirations of aboriginal peoples across Canada. Preceding the decision in *Sparrow,* the Supreme Court of Canada delivered several decisions which, at face value were indicative of a changing attitude. In several major cases (*Calder, Guerin, Simon* and *Sioui*), the Supreme Court ruled in favour of aboriginal litigants and against the Crown (the representative of the state). While each is important in its own right, none of the preceding cases matches the significance of *Sparrow.* George Erasmus, then chief of the Assembly of First Nations, called the *Sparrow* decision "an extremely major victory . . . we won big" (in Binnie 1990: 217).

This book will examine what exactly was "won." The issues and rights enunciated in *Sparrow* are applicable to all aboriginal peoples across Canada, but I will focus particularly on the situation in British Columbia, and specifically on the two major players in the dispute: the Department of Fisheries and Oceans and the Musqueam Indian Band. The study will examine the issues from the perspective of both litigants, with particular emphasis on what exactly was "won" by the Musqueam Indian Band, what those "winnings" mean for aboriginal peoples[1] in general and what the decision signifies about law and social transformation in particular.

Other important sources of data are recent court decisions dealing with aboriginal rights. I will examine court challenges that have attempted to take the *Sparrow* rights even further. For example, even though the Supreme Court ruled that aboriginal peoples had the first priority to harvest fish before any other users, the court did not decide whether that fish could be commercially sold. Recent court of appeal decisions from Ontario appear to favour an aboriginal commercial fishery, but the appellate courts in B.C. have ruled that an aboriginal right to a commercial fishery does not exist.

# Introduction

To receive an accurate picture of what is happening in the fishing waters of British Columbia, one must first wade through the lies, misinformation, heated rhetoric and political posturing that is being practised by all of those involved in the fishing industry, particularly by the commercial sector. The truth is there for anyone who seeks it, but still the untruths persist. An editorial in the *Vancouver Province* illustrates: "Since the native fisheries was expanded following court decisions enforced by Ottawa, the salmon available to commercial fishermen have dwindled alarmingly" (in Glavin 1993: 11).

# Chapter Two

# Aboriginal Fishing Rights before *Sparrow*

Not far from the Canadian border, the Makah Indian Band of Washington State recently applied for a license to hunt five grey whales for food and ceremonial purposes. The reaction was swift, yet predictably uninformed. The Sea Shepherd Society, a self-styled environmental group, (and other organizations) vowed to challenge the hunt if the license was approved. The overreaction reached into Canada, specifically British Columbia, which is fighting its own battle over fishing rights with aboriginal peoples. That the issue was not about fishing but about hunting a protected species in a foreign jurisdiction did not stop a local Vancouver newspaper from speculating on what might happen in Canada if aboriginal peoples made a similar application. No doubt, the newspaper was motivated by the continuing battles over fishing between the aboriginal peoples and the commercial fishing industry. The newspaper conducted an informal poll; 238 callers responded and 85 percent were firmly opposed to any notion of aboriginal hunting for whales (*Vancouver Province,* May 24, 1995). That this was an issue of the Makah Band attempting to revive and exercise a traditional activity was irrelevant. One apparently incensed caller declared that the proposed hunting was fine by him as long as "they did it in canoes they paddle." All this fuss and alarm was over a situation that had not even occurred in Canada.

Consider if you will the position of the federal government of Canada in a 1985 aboriginal hunting rights case. In *R.* v. *Simon,* the Crown argued that the right to hunt, as embodied in a 1752 treaty, was limited to hunting by methods in existence then. While one may dismiss the above anonymous caller as misinformed, what is one to make of the position of the federal government? Although *Simon* dealt with hunting rights, the similarities of the government's position on aboriginal fishing rights is noteworthy. The issue really boils down to which group gains from resource extraction or exploitation. To the court's credit, in *Simon* the judges dismissed the Crown's argument and confirmed the acquittal of the defendant.

The battle for aboriginal fishing rights is intertwined with the battle for the assertion and recognition of aboriginal rights. The two issues are not mutually exclusive and represent a complex part of the much larger struggle for self-government. At stake here is the survival of an ancient culture, traditions and a claim on an economically viable and a potentially self-sufficient way of life. The struggle for the recognition of aboriginal rights is a struggle for recognition as a people with a distinct and diverse culture. More importantly, it is a struggle for the control over the resources of their lands. The issue of aboriginal rights is complicated and contentious, and is as much political as legal. However, politically, the issue has been and continues to be a proverbial "hot potato" passed on by successive and different levels of governments that are reluctant to deal with it fairly and openly. The failure at the political level ultimately leaves the question for the courts to decide.

## ABORIGINAL RIGHTS

In order to understand the concept of aboriginal fishing rights, it is instructive to first consider what is meant by aboriginal rights. Even then the concept remains somewhat elusive. Until recently, little, if any, legal or political attention was given to the subject of aboriginal rights and, until the 1960s, aboriginal rights did not even merit academic commentary (*Financial Post* 1990; *R*. v. *Sparrow* 1990: 405).

In 1886, in one of the first court cases dealing with aboriginal rights, *St. Catherines Milling and Lumber Company* v. *The Queen,* Chancellor Boyd referred to "Indians" as "heathens and barbarians" with no "fixed abodes." Even though the case involved profound implications for aboriginal rights, the aboriginal peoples had no legal representation and, according to Kulchyski (1994: 22), were most likely unaware of the prosecution of the case. Aboriginal peoples, in any event, were of secondary importance. The real battle was between the federal and provincial governments to determine which government would derive financial benefits from lease of aboriginal lands to the St. Catherines Milling and Lumber Company. Upon appeal to the Judicial Committee of the Privy Council, which until 1949 was the final court of appeal from the Supreme Court of Canada, Lord Watson dismissed aboriginal rights as not deserving of consideration. He stated (in Kulchyski 1994: 21): "There was a great deal of learned discussion at the Bar with respect to the precise quality of aboriginal rights, but the lordships do not consider it necessary to express any opinion upon the point."

Prior to the *Constitution Act, 1982*, and the *Sparrow* decision, the highest court in the land had done little to address the question. The Supreme Court of Canada, almost without exception, ruled against aboriginal rights. As the court recently pointed out, for most of the twentieth century the rights of "Indians" to their aboriginal lands has been virtually ignored (*Sparrow* 1990).

In the absence of guidance by the Supreme Court of Canada, the various provincial courts confused the matter further by making inconsistent and contradictory rulings in their attempts to deal with the persistent issue of aboriginal rights. In a case involving consequences of the highest magnitude for aboriginal peoples, the Quebec Court of Appeal, in *Kanatewat et al.* v. *The James Bay Development Corporation and A.G. (Quebec),* declared that aboriginal rights were too vague to recognize (in Elliott 1991: 25).

The public reluctance to legally recognize, or even acknowledge, the existence of aboriginal rights mirrored the position of the provincial governments and the government of Canada, which did not recognize aboriginal claims as having any legal status (*Financial Post* 1990). In a 1969 discussion paper (in Sanders 1990: 714), the federal government proposed that all aboriginal land claims be rejected and recommended that both the treaties, and Indian special status, be phased out in order to completely assimilate aboriginal peoples into the Canadian mainstream. During the same period, the government of Quebec embarked on the massive James Bay hydroelectric project and the federal government proposed the MacKenzie Valley natural gas pipeline project, both massive undertakings that cut across traditional aboriginal lands. Typical of the attitude of the state, the aboriginal peoples were not even consulted, nor were they a factor in the decision to initiate the projects. The discussion paper proposals and the public projects mobilized Indian opposition and had the effect of reviving the struggle for the recognition of aboriginal rights (in Sanders 1990: 714).

The confusion surrounding aboriginal rights becomes even more compli-cated when one considers the situation in British Columbia. While the rest of Canada is more or less covered by treaties or other agreements or legal instruments, the terms of which have been generally ignored by the courts and successive governments, only fourteen treaties, covering mostly Vancouver Island, were signed in B.C. Most aboriginal peoples in B.C. never formally surrendered their lands through treaties, and their claims to traditional lands are premised on these unsurrendered aboriginal rights (Pearse 1982: 180).

In the early 1970s the government of Canada agreed to discuss land claims in B.C. on the condition that the various tribes form one negotiating team (Sanders 1990: 714). Having placed aboriginal peoples on reserves in remote and isolated regions of B.C., the government was now asking that they form a united team, a patently disingenuous move by the state in view of the diversity of the various tribes and differing interests and concerns, not to mention the wide geographical disbursement of a dispossessed peoples. Not surprisingly the attempt to form one unified negotiating team failed, and to this day the impasse continues.

Following the failure of the never-started land claims negotiations, the Nisga'a Tribal Council of B.C., led by Frank Calder, initiated court action seeking a declaration that they held aboriginal title to their traditional lands (Sanders 1990: 714). In the now famous case of *Calder* v. *Attorney-General of B.C.,* the chief justice of British Columbia, C.J.C. Davey, dismissed the Nisga'a's claims. He wrote (in Asch and MacKlem 1991: 501):

> [The Nisga'a] were at the time of settlement a very primitive people with few of the institutions of civilized society. I see no evidence to justify a conclusion that the aboriginal rights claimed by the successors of these primitive people are of a kind that it should be assumed the Crown recognized them when it acquired the mainland of British Columbia by occupation.

In other words, it was the court's view that whatever rights had been held by aboriginal peoples were no longer valid simply because the land had been settled and occupied by whites.

The decision was appealed to the Supreme Court of Canada in 1973. Even though the Supreme Court frowned upon the tone of the lower court ruling, it nevertheless dismissed the appeal. However, the Nisga'a Tribal Council celebrated a "victory." The majority of the court agreed that aboriginal title existed in law but could not decide whether the title claimed by the Nisga'a had been extinguished. Here for the first time was a recognition by the highest court in the land that aboriginal title had legal status.

Even though the *Calder* case has been cited for its legal significance, it is difficult to accord it much substantive merit. It is all fine and good to accord aboriginal title legal status, but what does that really mean? If aboriginal peoples had title to their traditional lands, could they then sell the land? Could they develop it? And if aboriginal title existed, where did it exist? Could it be applied in a tangible manner to an actual piece of real estate? The court opted out by not dealing with the issue of extinguishment and whether the Nisga'a had title. By sleight of hand and rhetorical appeasement, the court was able to satisfy all parties, especially the provincial government, which would most likely have had to pay out millions of dollars in compensation. The victory, however slight, for the Nisga'a was an end to a long battle, but it was a dubious victory because all that was "won" was an official recognition that they had never surrendered their aboriginal rights to their traditional lands.

However even this "victory" was considered by many, including aboriginal leaders, to be a "fluke," since, according to some, the decision served as a catalyst for the cancellation of the MacKenzie Pipeline, a negotiated settlement of the Quebec Hydro project and a reversal of the government proposals outlined in the 1969 discussion paper (in Sanders 1989: 716). The *Calder* decision also led to the initiation of land-claims negotiation between the federal government and the Nisga'a. As of the date of writing, the negotiations had been completed and a tentative agreement had been signed; however, the deal remains unratified by all parties—the federal and provincial governments and the Nisga'a.

Notwithstanding the recognition by the Supreme Court of Canada of the existence of aboriginal title, the waters surrounding the issue of aboriginal rights remained murky.

In 1978 the Liberal government of Pierre Trudeau announced that it would seek to repatriate the Canadian Constitution from its colonial "ruler," the United Kingdom. The announcement started a series of intense debates, lobbying and protests, including court challenges seeking to halt repatriation. That the new constitution was to include a charter of rights and freedoms generated even more debate. On this issue alone, over twelve hundred groups made representations to special parliamentary committees (Mahoney 1992: 228). The aboriginal organizations, mainly the National Indian Brotherhood (the NIB, now the Assembly of First Nations), were initially opposed to the enterprise and lobbied extensively against it (Mandel 1994: 249; Sanders 1990: 718).

In the first draft of the new constitution, aboriginal peoples were barely mentioned and no significant protection of aboriginal rights was included in other drafts. It appeared that aboriginal concerns were not going to be addressed at all while the federal government negotiated new constitutional arrangements with the provincial governments (*R. v. Agawa* 1988: 78; Mandel 1994: 249–50). However, the aboriginal organizations did not sit idly by.

> The major native organizations were not about to let this happen. They saw the constitutional turmoil [negotiations] as an opportunity to advance their claims to land and self-government. They launched a massive public relations attack on the whole *Charter* enterprise . . . the National Indian Brotherhood . . . (lobbied) British MPs against passage of the federal resolution . . . the Union of British Columbia Indian Chiefs chartered a train ("the Constitution Express") to take Indians from across the country to Ottawa and then on to the United Nations. (Sheppard and Valpy [1982: 167], in Mandel 1994: 249)

According to Mandel (1994), for some reason the aboriginal organizations had second thoughts and agreed to participate in the process. Following a culmination of intensive and sometimes divisive lobbying by aboriginal organizations, several amendments were included in the *Constitution Act, 1982* that specifically addressed aboriginal issues. The most important amendment is section 35(1), which states: "The existing aboriginal and treaty rights of the aboriginal peoples of Canada are hereby recognized and affirmed."

It is important to note that the aboriginal organizations also lobbied extensively to ensure that section 35(1) was placed outside the *Charter* and was therefore beyond the legislative reach of section 1, which allows infringement of constitutionally guaranteed rights if justifiable, and section 33, the overriding clause, of the *Charter*.

Having recognized aboriginal rights in section 35(1), the drafters of the constitution, however, left undefined what such rights meant. Instead, the drafters mandated a series of constitutional conferences to address the question. These televised and widely trumpeted conferences, which cost tens of millions of dollars, failed to resolve the matter. More importantly, their failure demonstrated the immense divide between aboriginal leaders and the provincial and federal governments, and they ended with increased acrimony. Aboriginal rights remained undefined. The vagueness of section 35(1) led one commentator to refer to it as an "empty shell" (see Barkin 1990: 307).

Law professor Brian Slattery, a leading constitutional expert, had this to say about section 35(1): "The sections regarding aboriginal rights leads us from darkness to darkness, in that they substitute impenetrable obscurity for what was formerly shadowy gloom" (1983: 232). And in a particularly prophetic statement he added, "They pose an unusually difficult task for a court, required, on the basis of only the most general of indicators, to resolve disputes of daunting historical and theoretical dimensions" (Slattery 1983: 232).

The question then is whether the Canadian courts are equipped to deal with section 35(1). These courts are by virtue of section 35(1) asked to protect aboriginal rights, which in the past they have ignored or viewed with considerable indifference and downright racist commentary. The courts are not only entrusted with defining what those rights are, but also with the task of protecting them.

According to Slattery, aboriginal rights refers to:

> a range of rights held by native peoples, not by virtue of Crown grant, agreement, legislation, but by reason of the fact that aboriginal peoples were once independent, self-governing entities, in possession of most of the lands making up Canada. (1983: 243)

Slattery's point, while morally principled, has not been embraced by the courts, and surely one cannot expect otherwise. For decades the Canadian courts have conveniently overlooked the undeniable historical fact that aboriginal settlement and possession of the lands now known as Canada preceded white settlement by a conservative estimate of at least 10,000 to 15,000 years (in Elliott 1991: 25). But what is fair and just has nothing to do with intricacies of legal arguments and legal reasoning, the sources of which emanate from English common law. It is worth noting that English common law principles were primarily for the protection of the property of the monied classes in pre-industrial England (Hay 1975). The transplanted legal system was never intended to deal with aboriginal issues in the first place. The limitations of the courts in looking beyond the parameters of their "creator" was unapologetically acknowledged in an American case, the principles of which hold true for Canada. Justice Marshall, in the 1823 case of *Johnson* v. *McIntosh,* stated (in Bartlett, 1990: 456):

> However extravagant the pretension of converting the discovery of an inhabited country into conquest may appear; if the principle has been asserted in the first instance, and afterwards sustained; if a country has been acquired and held under it; if property of the great mass of the community originates in it, it becomes the law of the land, and cannot be questioned.

According to Louise Mandell (1995: 4) the judges cannot truly answer the question "What are aboriginal rights?" bound as they are to act within the parameters of the Canadian legal system and the western concept of justice, which so far has resisted the very notion of aboriginal rights.

To understand or clarify the issue, it is essential to consider the aboriginal perspective, as expressed very eloquently by the Union of New Brunswick Indians (in Binnie 1990: 223):

> Aboriginal rights do include our hunting, fishing, trapping, and gathering as it relates to plant and animal life. Aboriginal rights include our right to exist as Indians, to govern ourselves, and to determine our livelihood, political, cultural, economic, social, and legal units. We have these rights and much more because we have never been conquered.

## THE FISHING INDUSTRY IN BRITISH COLUMBIA

The battle over fishing rights promises no easy victories, only bloody ones, for the stakes are high. That fishing is of vital national importance was underscored by the diplomatic row between Canada, Spain and the European Community, and between Canada and Alaska over salmon stocks. The fight to harvest fish stocks reached the point of armed confrontation when Canadian authorities boarded a Spanish trawler fishing off the coast of Newfoundland. The United Nations intervened, and Canada stood accused of bullying and gunboat diplomacy. That Canada was apparently on thin ground as far as international law was concerned was deemed irrelevant; furthermore, the fact that Canada had overfished the stocks to near extinction was not considered. Why accept responsibility when someone else can be blamed (see, for example, Simpson 1995a and 1995b)?

The fishing industry in Canada is a multibillion dollar business with an estimated worth of close to $3 billion. In British Columbia, the commercial fishery sector is the fourth largest primary industry, with an estimated worth of in excess of $1 billion. The fishery forms a vital part of the provincial economy, employing over 30,000 persons. It is the one industry in which aboriginal peoples find ready employment, as processors, cleaners and handlers, for the large corporations (Price Waterhouse 1989; British Columbia 1993). It is also the one industry in which aboriginal persons are economically active, holding about 20 percent of the commercial salmon licenses (DFO 1995: 15).

In Canada the major user and exploiter of the resource is the commercial industry dominated by multinational corporations. The Fisheries Council of British Columbia, a lobby group, represents the interests of the corporations that control fish processing in B.C.; these corporations also own and/or control the technologically advanced seine fleets that catch most of the fish. The seiners catch fish by dropping giant purse nets that encircle large areas and indiscriminately catch and kill everything in their path. The nets, by regulation, are limited to a length of 550 metres with an allowable depth of eighty or more metres.

These nets can be hauled up and their loads emptied and reset within thirty minutes. The seine fleets not only catch the most fish, but they also kill and discard tons of other fish and other species that are entangled in the nets. Much smaller in size and catching capacity are the gillnet and troll fleets used by individual commercial fishers. The trollers catch fish by dropping thickets of hooklines in deep water. In 1995 the troll fleet consisted of 1,500 boats, which caught 2.8 million salmon. The gillnetters catch fish by dropping mesh nets, which entangle them; in 1995 they caught 5 million salmon using 2,300 boats. Most, if not all, of the fish caught by the trollers and gillnetters are then sold to Fisheries Council of B.C. companies. The seine fleet, using 540 boats, caught 10.2 million salmon in 1995 (Howard 1996: D3; Alden 1996: A19; Glavin 1996c: 13; Greenpeace, in Anderson 1996; Ellis 1996). Another major user of fish is the sports and recreation industry, which plays an important role in tourism and has an estimated worth of approximately $1 billion (Cernetig 1995: 130). Vying for a foothold and a greater say in the management of fish and commercial participation are aboriginal communities across Canada (DFO 1995; Newell 1993; Glavin 1993).

Understandably, the various interest groups and users have a lot at stake, and the rights to harvest and exploit fish stocks are jealously guarded and fought over. The fight for access has pitted users against each other and the federal government, which has the constitutional authority to manage fisheries in Canada. The federal Department of Fisheries and Oceans is responsible for the management of fisheries, and this includes allocation of quotas to the various users, conservation of stocks, licensing of commercial fisheries and the management of various species, of which salmon is the most prized.

On the average, the commercial fishery is allocated the major share, at 94 percent of the salmon stock; the sports fishery is allocated 3 percent and aboriginal food fishery the remaining 3 percent (DFO 1995: 15). It is important to note that the "aboriginal food fishery" is a purely arbitrary distinction and a legal creation. It is a distinction not made by aboriginal peoples but by the government of Canada. In fact, the entire notion of a "food fishery" was created by government policy to accord the commercial fishery priority and ensure that aboriginal communities were able to feed themselves lest they become a burden on the public purse. Aboriginal participation in the commercial sector is on the basis of purchase of licenses, just the same as others in the commercial industry (in *Jack* v. *The Queen* 1980: 308–10).

When Professor Peter Pearse, head of the Commission on Pacific Fisheries Policy, submitted his report in 1982, he declared that the West Coast fisheries were at a crisis point, a result of misguided government policy, overfishing by all users both domestically and internationally, and "too many boats chasing too few fish." Dr. Pearse wrote (1982: vii): "[T]he economic circumstances of the commercial fisheries are exceptionally bleak . . . there is a growing concern about the precarious condition of many of our fish stocks and increasing anxiety among Indians about their traditional fishing rights."

A glance through recent newspaper headlines (see, for example, *Globe and Mail,* August 17, 1995: A2; *Vancouver Sun,* August 16, 1995: A1) indicates that not much has changed since 1995. Overfishing and depleted stocks have increased tension among the users, and one group in particular, a relatively powerless group holding only 3 percent of the salmon quota, has been particularly targeted by the commercial interests—the aboriginal fishers. The rationale for doing so may be to shirk responsibility for years of overfishing, greed, poor management and bungling DFO officials. It is much easier and convenient to blame a group that has already been effectively blamed in the past and stereotyped as plunderers. Perhaps the proper word to describe the calculated attacks on the aboriginal fishery is racism, pure and simple.

## ABORIGINAL FISHING RIGHTS

The battle over fishing rights is really a battle over a valuable commodity and resource. It is a battle between the powerful commercial industry and the aboriginal fishing communities who refuse to have their rights ignored and are asserting those rights with a persistence never seen before in Canada. Cunliffe Barnett, a provincial court judge in British Columbia, succinctly places the battle in perspective when he states (1995: 1): "My introduction to native fishing issues came during the summer of 1974 when I had to sentence the occasional native person for the illegal sale of food fish, an activity which I was told threatened the social order and the corporate well-being of B.C. Packers."

The aboriginal peoples of Canada had no legal rights unless those rights were specifically granted by statute or legislation (Sanders 1990). In order to understand the historic and legal significance of the *Sparrow* decision, it is crucial to understand that the Canadian courts, and the legal system, did not recognize any aboriginal right to fish. Aboriginal peoples could only fish at the behest of the government of Canada and in accordance with the terms set out in permits issued by the DFO. And as stated above, aboriginal peoples were only permitted to fish for food, and sale of food fish was legally prohibited. Even when fishing rights were expressly provided for in treaties, the courts either ignored those rights or held that provincial or federal laws regulating or restricting fishing were to be paramount—in spite of the terms of many treaties which placed the rights and benefits contained therein beyond the reach of legislative action (Pearse 1982: 179). Commissioner Pearse wrote (1982: 180): "I find these court decisions unsettling. It is hard to avoid the conclusion that they permit the government to unilaterally curtail the Indians' contractual rights embodied in treaties."

It is instructive to review two recent pre-*Constitution Act, 1982,* cases whose facts have remarkable similarities to those in *Sparrow.* In *R.* v. *Adolph* 1983, members of the Fountain Indian Band were convicted of fishing at a time prohibited by regulation. The accused had been fishing in traditional fishing waters on their reserve lands. They appealed their conviction to the British Columbia Court of Appeal (BCCA) on the basis that the exclusive aboriginal right to fish, granted to the Band, created a constitutional limitation on federal legislative powers in relation to aboriginal fisheries.[2] The accused argued that this fact alone would preclude the application of regulations to their fishing rights in the absence of a conservation need. The BCCA dismissed the appeal and upheld the conviction. The court refused to recognize any aboriginal right to fish and refused to grant legal standing to the DFO policy that aboriginal peoples had first priority for food fish, because government policy is not enforceable in a court of law. In this case, the government was not required to demonstrate that the closure of fishing was necessary for conservation because no aboriginal right had been established or recognized.

In another pre-constitution Supreme Court of Canada decision, in *R. v. Derriksan* (1976), the court declared that the aboriginal right to fish was governed by the *Fisheries Act* and regulations, and it upheld the conviction of the accused, notwithstanding the fact that he was fishing for food in traditional waters. In brief, prior to *Sparrow*, there was no legally recognized aboriginal right to fish; the *Fisheries Act* and regulations were paramount over the alleged needs or rights of any aboriginal fishery.

The Department of Fisheries and Oceans, however, as a matter of policy, accorded first priority to the aboriginal food fishery, subject only to the needs of conservation (DFO 1989). Although this may sound good on paper, the reality was anything but. The major point of contention that led to *Sparrow* was, and still is, a fundamental difference on how fishing is viewed.

Aboriginal people regard fishing as a right, as a part of their history, culture, religion and tradition practised from time immemorial. Aboriginal peoples resent the facts that government permission is required to exercise an inherent right and that this right is not recognized but has only the status of a mere policy that specifies when, where and how much fish to catch, and what to do with it once caught (Pearse 1982: 178). In submissions before the commission, the Union of B.C. Indian Chiefs summarized their position (in Pearse 1982: 177):

> We have also been legislated against, arrested or threatened with arrest for practising our harvest of resources. Since regulations, restrictions and policies have come into existence harassment has become a real problem. Harassment on Indian fishing increases as more policies are developed.

A second point of contention is the practical difficulty of exercising the accorded first priority. The DFO food fishery policy allows aboriginal peoples to fish for food in the rivers on their traditional lands. However, migrating salmon have to swim a formidable gauntlet of barriers before arriving at these rivers en route to their spawning grounds. Out in the ocean are the technologically superior modern fishing fleets with their fish-finding devices. Then there are natural predators and the sport fisheries. According to a finding by the commission on fisheries:

> Inevitably, the commercial and sport fisheries sometimes take too many fish to provide sufficient stocks for both needed escapement and the Indian fishery, and by the time this is known the only way to maintain the stocks is to constrain Indian fishing. (Pearse 1982: 177)

A third point of contention is the delineation of the allocated fish as a "food fishery." Aboriginal peoples view access to fisheries as an inherent aboriginal right, which means they should be able to do with the fish as they wish. Fish has never been viewed as merely food by aboriginal peoples. Fish was a major commodity of trade among the various tribes and has played an integral role in aboriginal culture, tradition and religious ceremonies. Restriction and limitation of access to fish and prohibition of sale are seen as unwarranted controls. To ensure a further degree of control, government policy required the removal of the snout and dorsal fin—a practice that was offensive to aboriginal peoples but was useful to law enforcers for identifying "aboriginal food fish" in the event of illegal sale. Persons caught buying, selling or having in possession aboriginal food fish could be criminally charged and prosecuted (Pearse 1982: 177).

In the early 1900s, even as the regulatory control on the aboriginal food fishery grew stricter and stricter, there was resentment among the authorities over what they apparently viewed as "special treatment." They felt aboriginal food fishing provision was "costing" an estimated $3 million annually. By the end of the First World War, senior officials at the DFO contemplated ending the food fishery altogether (Newell 1993: 67).

## ABORIGINAL COMMERCIAL FISHERY

How did it come about that an activity once engaged in without hindrance, an activity that formed the economic backbone of many coastal tribes, was now beyond the reach of peoples whose ancestors had practised the craft long before the coming of the European settlers?

As the commercial industry developed in British Columbia, the aboriginal peoples participated fully and actively. They were instrumental in making the venture an international success, which proved very lucrative for the dozens of canneries that sprung up along the coast. Entire tribes and family members were involved in the industry as operators of boats, fishers, cleaners and processors. In fact, the knowledge, expertise, labour and skills of the aboriginal peoples were prized by the cannery operators. The aboriginal peoples knew all the best locations to fish, they had developed the best and most efficient technology of catching fish and, most importantly, they fished in a manner consistent with conservation needs to ensure a continuing supply (Glavin 1995; Newell 1993).

However, much to the chagrin of the white cannery operators and the government, the aboriginal peoples continued to assert their independence and routinely defied government directives to obtain fishing licenses, asserting that it was their right to fish. This made them "unreliable" and constituted a threat to an industry concerned both with competition and with ensuring a dependable labour supply (Newell 1993: 46–98). In the long run, the aboriginal fishers became victims not only of racism but of their own success. As the market for fish grew, the demands placed on the stocks increased. To ensure sufficient supply for the commercial sector, the government simply reduced aboriginal fisheries (Copes 1995: 2). In an incisive treatise, Newell (1993) documents the deliberate manner in which the aboriginal peoples were brought under control by the industry and government and were eventually squeezed out and marginalized. The very peoples who had made the industry a success never stood a chance; the one industry in which aboriginal peoples had found success, and ready access to the new white economy, deliberately shut them out.

In summary, the explanation for the marginalization of the aboriginal commercial fishery is simple. As the economic value of fish increased, so did the interest of the white settlers. The increasing commercial value of fish resulted in a corresponding increase in the regulation and control of the aboriginal fishery. Aboriginal fishers, who were once encouraged to sell fish to the white settlers so as not to become an economic burden on the government, had now been prohibited from selling fish (Newell 1993; Pearse 1982: 177; DFO 1989).

## EVOLUTION OF REGULATORY POLICY
The history of colonialism and imperialism is a history created by the European powers and not by the vanquished. Indeed, recorded history remains the prerogative of those who have produced it. Unwritten, unacknowledged and little regarded has been the history of the vanquished. In British Columbia the history of the vanquished speaks of fishing in terms of reverence:

> The fishing has been of such importance that it is at the very roots of our cultures; our lives have revolved around the yearly arrival of the rivers' bounty. And so we cannot speak of the fishery without talking of our cultures because in many ways they are one and the same (Gitskan-Carrier Tribal Council, in Pearse 1982: 177).

The refusal and failure of the Canadian courts to recognize aboriginal fishing rights has been merely a reflection of other, almost countless, injustices meted out to the aboriginal peoples by the Canadian state. One writer, referring to a series of cases dealing with aboriginal issues, lamented this "sad history of national dishonour" (Palmer, in Pearse 1982: 180). With their own internal logic and penchant for obfuscation, the legal decision-makers ignored the undisputed historical fact that fish was an integral part of aboriginal life along the coastal and inland waters of B.C. Fish was not only a valuable source of food, but it was also revered in song and dance, and formed the economic and cultural lifeline of many tribes. Fish was a major commodity of trade among the various tribes, and later with the settlers and Hudson's Bay Company forts with the coming of the Europeans. According to anthropological evidence, the pattern of aboriginal settlement was, and continues to be, in large part determined by accessibility to fish (Dr. Barbara Lane (1980), in *Jack* v. *The Queen* 1980: 310). Fishing in general, and salmon fishing in particular, forms the very foundation of many aboriginal cultures. The importance of fishing to aboriginal peoples is underscored in various historical documents. Faced with the inevitability of increasing white settlement, the tribes that negotiated treaties with the colonial administrators in B.C. insisted on unhindered access to fish. Governor of Vancouver Island James Douglas negotiated fourteen treaties that included the following assurance (in DFO 1989: 4): "[that aboriginal peoples were] . . . at liberty to hunt over unoccupied lands and carry on [their] fisheries as formerly."

When British Columbia joined the confederation in 1871 to become part of the Dominion of Canada, there was no commercial fishery of any value. In that era, the colonial administration encouraged this aboriginal fishery in order to supply the food needs of the white settlers, whose time could then be devoted to agriculture. In addition, native peoples were encouraged to fish to avoid becoming a charge on the public purse (*Jack* v. *The Queen* 1980: 309).

Historically in Canada, whenever there was competition between the white settlers and aboriginal peoples, the government would wade in and tip the increasingly uneven playing field even more in favour of the whites. This is true not only of agricultural policies in the Prairies (see Carter 1990) but also of fishing. The current situation regarding aboriginal fisheries is the outcome of more than a century of policy development (Pearse 1982: 175). It is instructive to note that competition between white settlers and aboriginal peoples for agricultural lands led to the creation of Indian reserves. Even the process of dispossession or "reservization" recognized the importance of fishing not only to the aboriginal peoples but to the white settlers. Therefore, the boundaries of the reserves generally coincided with traditional fishing areas. This served a twofold purpose: aboriginal peoples could continue their tradition of fishing, which in turn was also used for trade with the white community, providing food for the settlers (Lane [1980], in *Jack* v. *The Queen* 1980: 307).

Before 1877 there were no regulations of any type concerning fisheries in B.C. According to Rueben Ware ([1978], in Pearse 1982: 176):

> In this era there was no distinction between "food fishing" and commercial fishing. There was no regulation, no proclamations, no OICs [Orders in Council], no laws of any kind which specifically restricted or regulated Indian fishing in B.C.

# Aboriginal Fishing Rights Before *Sparrow*

In response to the development of the commercial fishing and canning industries, the Parliament of Canada enacted the *Dominion Fisheries Act* in 1877. This act did not affect aboriginal fisheries but provided legislative delegatory powers to the provinces from which to issue regulations. Ten years later, and again in response to the continuing development of commercial fishing, the province of British Columbia issued regulations effectively limiting aboriginal fishing for food and restricting sale or trade (Pearse 1982: 176; *Jack* v. *The Queen* 1980: 308–10). The British Columbia Fisheries Regulation, issued November 26, 1888, stated: "Indians shall, at all times, have liberty to fish for ... food for themselves, but not for sale, barter or traffic by any means other than with drift nets, or spearing."

This regulation marked the beginning of the end of a traditional way of life for the aboriginal peoples. Here for the first time was an explicit law restricting and defining fishing as for food only and to be done using only certain types of equipment, and specifically making it illegal for aboriginal fishers to sell their catch.

Six years later, in 1894, more regulations were introduced, imposing even further controls over aboriginal life. For the first time, aboriginal peoples were required to obtain permits from the authorities in order to fish for food. In 1910, additional regulations were issued, allowing the authorities to specify the area and time of fishing, as well as the type of equipment to be used. And in 1917 it became an offence to sell and buy fish caught under the provisions of fish permits (in *Jack* v. *The Queen* 1980: 310; Pearse 1982).

The development of the commercial fishing industry, the concomitant conflict between whites and aboriginal peoples, and the corresponding evolution of increasingly restrictive regulations for aboriginal fisheries is summed up by the Supreme Court of Canada in the *Jack* case (1980: 310):

> [T]he Regulation of 1888 came into effect at a period of growth in the fishing industry and on the threshold of great expansion in the British Columbia fishery ... [this] gave rise to [conflicts] between the Indians ... and the sport [and] commercial fishermen ... the [Regulations] became increasingly strict in regard to the Indian fishery over time, as first the commercial fishery developed and then sport fishing became common. What we can see is an increasing subjection of the Indian fishery to regulatory control. First, the regulation of the use of drift nets, then the restriction of fishing to food purposes, then the requirement of permission ... [and] ultimately, in 1917, the power to regulate even food fishing.

The preceding describes the legal and substantive situation, with minor variations to allow for changes in DFO policy, as it existed before the *Sparrow* decision.

## CONCLUSION

There is no doubt that increasing regulatory control of aboriginal fishing was, and is, a form of control over aboriginal life. The effective denial of and control of access to what aboriginal peoples consider their inherent right has resulted in resentment and acrimony not only among aboriginal peoples, but also among the different levels of government and other users of the resource.

The aboriginal struggle for complete participation in, and access to, fisheries is not about seeking special privileges, as the commercial industry (i.e., B.C. Fisheries Survival Coalition and the Fisheries Council of B.C.) argues. It is simply an attempt to recover and exercise, without hindrance, a fundamental and vital part of aboriginal culture and a way of life that decades of government control have effectively marginalized and decimated but failed to conquer. It is an attempt to recover a centuries-old economic activity that will allow aboriginal access to mainstream Canada. In submissions before the Commission on Fisheries, the members of the Nuu-chah-nulth Tribal Council stated:

> Participation in the fishing industry allowed us to remain living by the sea with our own people. And it was the kind of work that was more compatible with our way of life than other kinds of work in the white man's economy. It was . . . the lesser of two evils. It did not require us to give up our communities and our culture. (in Pearse 1982: 151)

In spite of the regulations, policies, criminal prosecution, threats and animosity, aboriginal peoples have defiantly refused to surrender their inherent rights. And it was this belief in the inherent right to a traditional way of life that led Ronald Sparrow, Jr., in open and deliberate defiance of the law, to cast his nets in the waters of Canoe Passage in the Fraser River where his ancestors from time immemorial had done so.

# Chapter Three

# The *Sparrow* Decision

In the annals of constitutional law and aboriginal rights, no Supreme Court of Canada case generated as much interest as the *Sparrow* decision did when it was pronounced in 1990. To this day, its implications continue to reverberate throughout the fishing industry. Some have described the decision as "phenomenal," and some have called it "historic." Some claim the decision created an aboriginal commercial fishery, while others claim that it did nothing of the sort. Some critics have stated that *Sparrow* decided nothing and have severely criticized the federal government for its "overreaction" and "acquiesence to the native agenda." Some aboriginal leaders celebrated the claim that "we won big," and some have wryly noted the continuance of the status quo (Binnie 1990; Elliott 1991; Duncan 1995; M. Smith 1995). In a particularly vehement attack on *Sparrow,* lawyer N.D. Mullins wrote a letter to the editor of *The National,* the official publication of the Canadian Bar Association; he dismissed the aboriginal position as "the absurd and unacceptable claims, demands, threats, and lies of Indians in Canada" and concluded: "[The] Indians lost the *Calder* case in every court in Canada [and] *Sparrow* decided nothing except that there should be a retrial to see whether the Indians could prove that they had aboriginal fishing rights prior to 1982" (in Barnett 1995: 1).

Why the ambivalence? The answer is complicated, because *Sparrow* is all that it is said to be and more. At first glance, *Sparrow* is about one person's defiance of the *Fisheries Act* and his assertion that fishing is an aboriginal right. To peoples accustomed to losing battles in the courts, it was a significant legal victory.

Clearly, the legal implications of the decision were profound and far-reaching. *Sparrow* is about many things: defiance; equality; access to a valuable natural resource; participation in a multibillion dollar industry; the revival and survival of tradition; and legal theft and denial. It is also about David against Goliath; and about racism, equality, justice, fairness and more. Perhaps most importantly, for the aboriginal peoples it is about the possibility of building a viable economic base upon which to base the ultimate achievement of self-government.

## BACKGROUND TO THE DECISION

The events leading to *Sparrow* had been preceded by increasing acrimony and hostility between the DFO and the Musqueam Indian Band.

Under the system of regulatory control in existence since 1917, the food fish catch of the Musqueam Indian Band had become marginal or non-existent. The

Band's food fish requirements were fulfilled by its members who held commercial fishing licenses (*Sparrow* 1990: 397). It was apparent that the DFO policy of according first priority to the aboriginal food fishery, subject only to conservation requirements, existed on paper only and was not implemented in fact. According to a former "native beat" reporter for the *Vancouver Sun*, Terry Glavin, the DFO's primary concern, as it had been from day one, was ensuring that the needs of the powerful commercial fishery were met first (Glavin 1995).

In 1978 an experimental system was introduced, which allowed the Musqueam to fish for a greater number of days than other users, with a larger net at a length of seventy-five fathoms. Under this scheme the number of Band members fishing increased from nineteen to sixty-four, and the number of boats increased from fifteen to thirty-eight. In 1978 the recorded catch of the Musqueam numbered 4,998 pieces, but by 1982 the recorded catch increased to 51,850 pieces (*Sparrow* 1990: 397; *Sparrow* 1987: 311). According to Bill Duncan (1995), senior program officer for the DFO, the department became alarmed not only at the size of the catch but at what also became apparent—that the fish was headed for the black market. The DFO's fears were borne out when it conducted a "sting" operation. In September 1982, undercover DFO agents purchased over 5,500 pieces of fish from members of the Musqueam Indian Band; the dorsal fin and snouts of the fish had been removed, indicating that Band members were selling fish caught under the provisions of their food fish license. Shortly thereafter, an early-morning, police-style raid was conducted on the Musqueam reserve; vehicles belonging to members of the Band were seized and charges were laid. However, all the charges against the members of the Band were dismissed and the vehicles were ordered returned on the grounds that their seizure had been unlawful.

It is not clear whether the next step taken by the DFO occurred as a result of the botched raid or had been planned beforehand, but the DFO ordered that the net length be reduced from seventy-five to twenty-five fathoms. Prior to the decree, the DFO had held discussions with the Musqueam Indian Band but had failed to reach a consensus on the size of the nets. The Band registered its protest and the DFO ordered the reduction in the size of the net. The DFO maintained that the net reduction was necessary to reduce the size of the catch. It felt that the seventy-five-fathom net was unreasonably large in relation to legitimate food requirements of the Band and was detrimental to conservation management. The Musqueam, in contrast, maintained that the net reduction had nothing to do with conservation and everything to do with "vindictiveness" on the part of the DFO officials due to the failure and subsequent embarrassment over the dismissal of charges that had arisen out of the "sting" operation (*Sparrow* 1987: 310–13). During the same period, the commercial sector continued to fish without restriction, further raising the ire of the Musqueam and providing credence to their view that the net restriction was in fact undue interference and not connected to conservation (Becker 1995).

# The *Sparrow* Decision

In 1983, using the twenty-five-fathom net, the recorded catch of the Musqueam Indian Band declined to 11,224 pieces. In 1984, in an atmosphere of increasing acrimony, the Band and the DFO again entered discussions regarding the conditions of the food fishing license for the upcoming season. These negotiations were characterized by Chief Becker as an exercise in futility because the DFO was not interested in the Musqueam point of view. The Band maintained that no restrictions should be imposed, but it also suggested that if any were imposed, a fifty-fathom net size would be acceptable. The DFO disagreed and again ordered the net length not to exceed twenty-five fathoms (*Sparrow* 1987: 310–13).

In a strategy meeting, the Musqueam Indian Band Council resolved to continue its defiance of the DFO. It was the avowed intent of the Band to defy the DFO by every possible means, including selling the fish they caught. The Musqueam did not consider their actions illegal. According to them, it was an exercise of an aboriginal right. During these events, the Musqueam Indian Band was quite aware of the recent passage into law of the *Constitution Act, 1982* and, according to Chief Joe Becker, were looking for an opportunity to test the implications of the protection accorded to aboriginal rights by section 35(1). The position of the DFO in restricting the size of the net, and in its continual regulation and harassment of aboriginal fishers, had provided that opportunity (Becker 1995).

In the late spring of 1984, some two years after the proclamation of the *Constitution Act, 1982*, several members of the Musqueam Indian Band were caught fishing in the Fraser River with illegal nets. One of those charged was Ronald Edward Sparrow, Jr. In a strategy meeting, the Band Council and legal counsel reviewed the cases of all those who had been charged, and decided that the case against Mr. Sparrow, although not considered the best case, provided the best circumstances upon which to launch a constitutional challenge. The Band had been systemically preparing for this day. All the details had been carefully planned, right down to its choice of legal counsel. The counsel was to be someone who believed in aboriginal rights and shared the Band's position: Marvin Storrow, who had been named to the honourary position of Queen's counsel by his peers.

Sparrow was charged under the *Fisheries Act* for fishing with a net longer than permitted by the terms of the Band's food fishing license. He did not deny the facts of the allegations. In his defence, he stated he had been exercising an existing aboriginal right protected by section 35(1) of the *Constitution Act, 1982*. This was a clear, deliberate and unequivocal challenge to the authority of the DFO. Here, like other aboriginal peoples who had done similar things in the past without success, was an aboriginal person asserting that the government of Canada had no right, jurisdiction or authority to interfere with, regulate, legislate or control in any way an aboriginal right.

At trial, Sparrow was convicted; the provincial court judge determined that an aboriginal right to fish had not been established, and held section 35(1) to be inapplicable. Sparrow appealed his conviction to the county court, which dismissed his appeal and upheld the conviction. Sparrow's further appeal to the British Columbia Court of Appeal was allowed. This court overturned the conviction and ordered a new trial.

Although the BCCA decided the case in Sparrow's favour and ordered a new trial, its decision was inconclusive and left many issues unresolved. For example, the court found that Sparrow was, at the time of the alleged offence, exercising an existing aboriginal right that had not been extinguished. However the court also held that the restriction on the length of the net was not inconsistent with section 35(1). In other words, Sparrow could not claim section 35(1) protection. A new trial ordered on this basis would have resulted in a conviction, because Sparrow had been charged with fishing with an illegal net, a fact he did not deny.

Perhaps the most important aspect of the BCCA decision was the finding that the aboriginal food fishery was entitled to constitutional protection, and that protection, with the exception of conservation measures, gave aboriginal fisheries first priority over the interests of other users, including commercial fisheries.

This was indeed an almost revolutionary statement. For a Canadian court to declare that the economic interests of a major industry were less deserving of consideration than those of aboriginal peoples had been almost unheard of. According to Michael Hunter (1995), president of the Fisheries Council of B.C., the fishing industry was taken by surprise. The decision was unexpected and created a stir on the waterfront. That this decision brought to the forefront decades of simmering hostilities and racist sentiment from the mainly white commercial fishery was no surprise. Michael Hunter, a relatively recent arrival from the distant shores of England, declared aboriginal fishing rights to be "un-Canadian" and "obnoxious and invalid" (in Glavin 1993: 8). Clearly the industry felt threatened.

In view of the interests at stake, it was not surprising that the BCCA decision was appealed. For different reasons, both Mr. Sparrow and the Crown (representing the federal government) appealed and cross-appealed to the Supreme Court of Canada. The National Indian Brotherhood intervened in support of Sparrow. And the Crown intervenors amounted to a virtual massing of the troops: the B.C. Wildlife Federation, the Fisheries Council of B.C., the United Fishermen and Allied Workers Union, and the provincial governments of Ontario, Quebec, B.C., Saskatchewan, Alberta and Newfoundland were all granted intervenor status in support of the Crown.

The court case had all the makings of a classic showdown. It was David against Goliath, and many of the spectators sided with Goliath, including a number of First Nations. According to Becker (1995), there was little support for the Musqueam court challenge among other aboriginal Bands. The Bands expressed concern and fear, which was not without reason, that the court challenge would not succeed and would result in a setback and increased curtailment of whatever rights, albeit undefined, that continued to exist.

## THE APPEAL ARGUMENTS

Ronald Sparrow appealed on the grounds that the BCCA had erred in the following findings (in *Sparrow* 1990: 392):

> (1) in holding that s. 35(1) . . . protects the aboriginal right only when exercised for food purposes and permits restrictive regulation of such rights (for conservation purposes or in the public interest);
>
> (2) in failing to find that the net length restriction . . . was inconsistent with s. 35(1).

The Crown cross-appealed on several grounds, arguing that the BCCA had erred in making the following findings of fact and law (in *Sparrow* 1990: 392):

> (1) that the aboriginal right had not been extinguished;
>
> (2) in finding that Mr. Sparrow possessed an aboriginal right to fish for food;
>
> (3) that the aboriginal right to fish for food also included the right to take fish for ceremonial and societal needs;
>
> (4) that the Band now enjoyed a constitutionally protected priority over the rights of other users.

The irony in the position of the Crown, in cross-appealing the BCCA decision, was quite remarkable and in sharp contrast with the comments of various courts in Canada. The courts have ruled, or stated, that the relationship between the Crown and the aboriginal peoples is trustlike, not adversarial, that the Crown has a "fiduciary responsibility" to the aboriginal peoples and that no sharp dealing should be sanctioned, because the honour of the Crown is at stake (*Sparrow* 1990). However profound or well-meaning the words of the Courts may have been, they obviously were not heeded, particularly when the stakes were as high as they were in *Sparrow.*

The Crown, backed by the full support of the commercial industry and several provincial governments, opposed every issue that was fundamental to the exercise of the aboriginal right as decided by the BCCA. It is telling that one of the cases that the Crown relied upon to support its position was none other than the *St. Catherines Milling* decision, without doubt a most blatant piece of racist judicial reasoning. The Crown argued that the BCCA was wrong in recognizing the existence of an aboriginal right to fish and maintained that there was no aboriginal right to fish for food. In covering all bases, the Crown asserted that even if an aboriginal right had existed, it had been extinguished in view of the history of regulatory control of the aboriginal fishery. That the regulatory impositions were at the behest of commercial interests was irrelevant and not acknowledged by the Crown. The Crown also objected to the finding by the BCCA that aboriginal peoples had a right to fish not only for food but also for ceremonial reasons and to fulfil societal needs. The Crown appeared most affronted, almost aghast, at the BCCA's finding that the aboriginal access to fish, which before had been meted out as a privilege by the state, was now regarded as an aboriginal right and accorded constitutional protection and priority. The Crown argued that the aboriginal fishery deserved no such priority, and it maintained that section 35(1) did not invalidate regulation based on overriding public interest, such as the needs of other users.

However, the greatest fear, as demonstrated by the numerous intervenors representing the fishing industry and the provincial governments, was that the aboriginal right could be extended to commercial fishing.

## THE SUPREME COURT OF CANADA DECISION

When the Supreme Court of Canada (SCC) had decided the *Sparrow* case, little did it know the consternation the decision would cause. The SCC dismissed both the appeal and cross-appeal; it upheld Mr. Sparrow's acquittal and ordered that a new trial be held in accordance with the analysis of section 35(1) set out in the decision.

At its most basic level the SCC agreed with the BCCA, but what the court had to say about section 35(1) sent shock waves across the nation. It had taken the highest court eight long years, but here finally was its first detailed look at section 35(1). What the politicians had failed to define and resolve had been given some teeth by the court. Whether the bite proved effective will be examined later. The SCC examined section 35(1) at length and set out an analytic framework or "test," according to which section 35(1) must be interpreted by all courts where the protection of aboriginal rights are at issue. George Erasmus, then chief of the Assembly of First Nations, declared the *Sparrow* decision "an extremely major victory . . . we won big" (in Binnie 1990: 217).

When section 35(1) was included in the *Constitution Act, 1982*, many commentators had viewed the section as an "empty box" to be filled with explicit provisions by later negotiations (in Cassidy 1990: 4). That these negotiations, in the form of mandated constitutional conferences, resolved nothing and were a dismal failure came as no surprise to those on the left of the political spectrum (see Mandel 1994: 353–69). It had also come as no surprise that the federal government, throughout the BCCA hearing and before the SCC, had argued that section 35(1) was of a merely preambular nature. In other words, a section for which aboriginal organizations had lobbied long and hard had been dismissed by the government as simply a mere statement without legal effect.

Both the BCCA and the SCC disagreed emphatically with the government's position; the SCC cited the BCCA when the judges stated: "[T]o so construe s. 35(1) would be to ignore its language and the principle that the Constitution should be interpreted in a liberal and remedial way . . . s. 35(1) is a solemn commitment that must be given meaningful content (*Sparrow* 1990: 407–08.

That the solemn commitment was vehemently argued against by federal lawyers with the full support of the provinces and commercial interests indicates clearly that the aboriginal rights promised in the Canadian Constitution were never really intended to take on a substantive role. How else can we explain the failure of the constitutional conferences over a century of land-claims negotiations? How else can we explain that resource extraction plays second fiddle to none, least of all to aboriginal peoples? How else can we explain the political reluctance and unwillingness to even address aboriginal issues? How else can we explain the last-minute nature of the inclusion of an aboriginal rights clause in the constitution?

In this respect the SCC must be accorded full marks. The judges (*Sparrow* 1990: 406) noted that section 35(1) became a reality after "a long and difficult struggle in both the political forum and the courts" and it is not to be taken lightly. The court held that the constitutionalization of aboriginal rights demanded that the issue be viewed seriously. The SCC stated:

> The nature of s. 35(1) itself suggests that it be construed in a purposive way. When the purposes of the affirmation of aboriginal rights are considered, it is clear that a generous, liberal interpretation of the words in the constitution is demanded. (*Sparrow* 1990: 407)

## WHAT THE SUPREME COURT OF CANADA DECIDED

The Supreme Court of Canada reviewed the history and litany of injustices meted out to the aboriginal peoples and acknowledged: "We cannot recount with much pride the treatment accorded to the native peoples of this country" (*Sparrow* 1990: 404). In essence the SCC dismissed all of the substantive arguments of the Crown. However, the court could afford to do so and appear generous in its approach because the actual effect of the decision was a limitation of the recognized aboriginal right.

There is no doubt that the SCC decision in *Sparrow* is one of great legal significance. It has been the strongest signal yet from the highest court in the land that aboriginal rights must be taken seriously, and that the issues raised demand answers. The SCC made it clear that such answers are best resolved by negotiations, and that a high standard of conduct is expected of the government.

The SCC ruled that Ronald Sparrow was, at the time of the alleged offence, exercising an existing aboriginal right to fish for food, a right that had not been extinguished notwithstanding nearly one century of increasingly strict regulatory control. The SCC also stated that government regulation and policy was incapable of delineating, defining or limiting that right. It ruled that where it is argued that an aboriginal right has been extinguished, the extinguishment must have been clearly and plainly intended. The SCC also upheld the BCCA's expansive interpretation of the food fishery to include fishing for societal and ceremonial needs.

Perhaps the most important legal victory for Mr. Sparrow and the Musqueam Indian Band was the SCC affirmation of the BCCA ruling that the aboriginal fishing right was a constitutionally protected right, which is to be accorded top priority over the needs of other users, subject only to conservation. The ruling by the SCC does not mean that the aboriginal fishery cannot be regulated; in this respect the power and jurisdiction of Parliament is supreme. However, the SCC clearly circumscribed that power by holding that the state must justify any regulation that may affect the aboriginal right. If the justification is for valid reasons, such as conservation, then the brunt of any conservation measures must be borne by the other user groups, such as the commercial and sports fishery sector. The court also held that any regulation that has the effect of interfering with an aboriginal right must occur only if it does not cause undue hardship to the person exercising that right. Finally, the court ruled that the government must consult with aboriginal peoples on any regulation that may affect their fishing rights.

Legally, and theoretically, there can be no denying that the decision dealt a severe blow to the government, and to the DFO in particular. In essence, the SCC told the government that they could no longer bully aboriginal fishers. The DFO still has the constitutional authority to manage fisheries, including the regulation of the aboriginal fishery. But the complete and arbitrary control exercised by the government over the aboriginal fishery was declared invalid.

However, the story does not end here. No matter now positive the ruling or directives of a court may be, it requires action on part of the "loser" to demonstrate in a tangible manner that the directives of the court are being carried out. As we shall see later, the spirit of the SCC ruling has not been carried out. In subtle and insidious ways, the DFO has maintained control over the aboriginal fishery and continues to ignore in practice the court's decision that the aboriginal fishery is to be accorded top priority.

## WHAT THE SUPREME COURT OF CANADA DID NOT DECIDE

Although the legal issues adjudicated upon in *Sparrow* are significant, what is more significant, and conspicuous by its obvious exclusion, is what the Supreme Court did not decide. The SCC did not rule on whether aboriginal peoples, or the Musqueam Indian Band in particular, had a right to sell the fish they caught.

As far as legal technicalities, common law, rules and procedures are concerned, the SCC was legally correct in not ruling on the commercial aspects of the aboriginal fishery. The court challenge was never presented on a commercial basis, i.e., that the aboriginal fishery included a right to sell fish. The question before the court was whether the net-length restriction was constitutional in view of section 35(1). The Musqueam Indian Band that took the *Sparrow* case to the Supreme Court was wary of presenting a commercial rights argument to the courts because it would have seemed that the Musqueam were trying to grab too big a piece of the pie. *Sparrow* was a cautious step forward to test the waters of section 35(1); it should be remembered that Mr. Sparrow's case was not the best case the Band could have hoped for, but, according to legal advice, it was the only case that presented the logical basis upon which to test the strength of the constitutional protection of this section.

Notwithstanding legal technicalities and common law principles, there had been absolutely nothing preventing the SCC from ruling on the issue. In other words, the SCC could have ruled that the Musqueam Indian Band had a right to sell their fish. The court could have said that the rules imposed upon the aboriginal fishery, and the arbitrariness of those rules, were inconsistent with section 35(1). The court, after all, did agree with the BCCA in extending the privilege of food fishing to constitutional status and protection, and the court further extended that right to include the taking of fish for "societal and ceremonial needs." But the court was under no obligation to extend the concept of "food fishing" to encompass other uses that were and are integral to the Musqueam Band because this issue was not raised in the appeal to the BCCA. One cannot help but surmise that the court could afford to be generous in expanding the food fishery because the effect was actually to limit aboriginal fishing to parameters conducive to control. By not including the commercial aspect, the court implicitly made it clear that the aboriginal right to fish did not include the right to sell fish.

The judges sitting on the bench of the Supreme Court are not naive. They knew that the Musqueam had existed as a society long before the coming of European settlers, and that the Musqueam had traded and bartered in fish with other coastal and inland tribes and, later, with the Europeans. They knew that fish formed an integral part of the economy of not only the Musqueam but other coastal peoples in B.C. And, yet, the court declined to address the issue, taking refuge behind legal rules.

Why should the Supreme Court have said "yes" to an aboriginal fishery that included the sale of fish? First and foremost, it would have been a truly just and fair settlement. After all, the court did admonish the justice system and Canadian society for being unable to recount with pride the treatment accorded to aboriginal peoples. The merit for recognizing a commercial component to the aboriginal fishery is found in explicit statements by the court throughout its decision. By extending the food fishery to include the taking of fish for societal needs, the court had a clear opening upon which to conclude that societal needs could mean a right to do what the Musqueam had done with the fish before being legally prohibited from doing so—mainly trade and barter. If the court accords a legal right to include "societal needs," should not those needs be defined by those to whom it is accorded? Societal needs were not defined by either the BCCA or the SCC; arguably those needs could mean commercial activity, which would benefit the aboriginal society as a whole by addressing some of its most pressing social problems such as poverty, unemployment and dependence on social assistance. The definition of societal needs is only limited by one's imagination, and it is apparent that the SCC suffered from a remarkable lack of imagination on that day.

There is still further support for the economic use of fish by the Musqueam in the decision. For example, the Supreme Court states: "[T]he phrase 'existing aboriginal rights' must be interpreted flexibly so as to permit their evolution over time . . . [and] suggests that those rights are affirmed in a contemporary form rather than in their primeval simplicity and vigour" (*Sparrow* 1990: 397).

This statement provides clear support for reviving the ancient practice of barter and trade into its modern-day equivalent of open market sale. It also includes a recognition that aboriginal fishers should be allowed to exercise that right by use of modern equipment and not only "in boats they paddle" or, as the Crown argued in *Simon,* in the way they did in the 1700s.

With regard to aboriginal fishery, the BCCA *(Sparrow* 1987: 331) stated:

> The breadth of the right should be interpreted liberally in favour of the Indians. So "food purpose" should not be confined to subsistence. In particular, this is so because the Musqueam tradition involves . . . a broader use of fish than mere day-to-day consumption.

The SCC, in an earlier aboriginal rights case, *Nowegijick* v. *The Queen,* had stated that treaties and statutes should be liberally construed, and doubtful expressions should be resolved in favour of aboriginal peoples. The SCC applied the same principle of liberal rhetoric to section 35(1) and concluded that its constitutional nature means a "generous and liberal interpretation is demanded."

Well then, if a "generous" application is demanded, why not a recognition of the commercial nature of aboriginal fishery? And if one really thinks about it, there is no requirement for generosity but rather for justice and fairness when the issue is about the restoration of rights once enjoyed by the aboriginal peoples before the coming of white settlers. Being just and fair is not generous, it is simply doing the right thing. However, the principles enunciated, and the bold nature of the statements by the Supreme Court, amount to naught given their technical avoidance of the issue. The undeniable fact is that it would have taken a remarkable degree of courage on the part of the court to allow aboriginal fisheries an unhindered access to the resource. By unhindered, I mean a true recognition of the aboriginal right to do with the fish as they wish. Such a bold and courageous move on the part of the court would have turned the industry upside down. And the SCC was not blind to the magnitude of the economic implications. The judges stated:

> The presence of numerous intervenors representing the commercial fish interests . . . indicate the possibility of conflict between aboriginal fishing and the competitive commercial fishing . . . we recognize the existence of this conflict and the probability of its intensification as fish availability drops, demand rises, and tensions increase. (*Sparrow* 1990: 403)

On this account the SCC was not quite correct—there is not a *possibility* of conflict between aboriginal fisheries and commercial fishery, there *is* conflict already. In fact, there is a great deal of conflict and animosity (which is the subject of Chapter Four). Before moving on, it is important to discuss the "justification" scheme imported into section 35(1) by the Supreme Court.

## LIMITATION OF ABORIGINAL RIGHTS UNDER SECTION 35(1)

Before the passage of the *Constitution Act, 1982*, aboriginal organizations lobbied extensively to ensure that section 35(1) was placed beyond the reach of sections 1 and 33 of the *Charter*. Section 1 allows for the infringement of constitutionally guaranteed rights if it can be justified according to a test delineated in the SCC decision *R. v. Oakes,* and section 33 allows legislative action to override the *Charter* guarantees. The very thing aboriginal organizations feared, and with very good reason, occurred in *Sparrow*. In a subtle and almost insidious manner, the court imported into its analysis of section 35(1) a justification test, to allow for the limitation or control of aboriginal rights where none had been envisioned or intended by Parliament.

Where did this limitation come from? In commenting on the BCCA decision which had originally placed a limitation on s.35(1) rights, (for conservation purposes or in the public interest), Tom Berger (1989) former justice of the Supreme Court of British Columbia, declared that the court had "invented it out of thin air" (606). This limitation was upheld and detailed by the Supreme Court of Canada which, in essence, ruled that aboriginal rights could be curtailed according to a justificatory scheme. Several commentators (Freedman 1994; Mandel 1994; Elliott 1991; Binnie 1990) have argued that the limitation placed upon section 35(1) may have the effect of curtailing other aboriginal rights. The issue of particular concern here is that the decision was delivered by a fairly liberal and sympathetic court led by the renowned Chief Justice Dickson. What are successive courts to make of this, particularly in view of the fact that the members currently on the bench of the SCC are known for their conservative values? In *Sparrow*, the SCC has provided successive courts an opening or scheme for controlling aboriginal rights, since the power of argument and legal obfuscation can be easily manipulated to support a variety of positions no matter how untenable or implausible they may be. Chief Joe Becker is blunt and readily acknowledges that the present make-up of the SCC does not bode well for future challenges under section 35(1); he further acknowledges that had *Sparrow* been presented to the SCC today, the result would have been even less favourable.

While reaching out to the aboriginal peoples of Canada, the SCC, with remarkable incredulity, does not appear cognizant of the paradoxical nature of its own statements. As noted earlier, the court concluded that the relationship between the state and aboriginal peoples should be trustlike; yet the relationship continues to be adversarial, as it has always been. The court acknowledges this point: "Our history has shown . . . that Canada's aboriginal peoples are justified in worrying about government objectives that may be superficially neutral but which constitute de facto threats to the existence of aboriginal rights and interests" (*Sparrow* 1990: 409). If this is so, then why not alleviate those concerns by not limiting section 35(1) rights? Perhaps because the judiciary is a construction of the state and is unable to dissociate from the ideological underpinnings of its creator.

## CONCLUSION

At first glance, *Sparrow* appears to have been an unqualified victory for the aboriginal peoples. However, upon sober reflection, the decision is anything but. There is no denying that the decision is of considerable legal significance, but that has not translated into any substantial benefit for the aboriginal peoples. Perhaps there is a moral victory, the value of which cannot be measured at this time.

The fact remains that *Sparrow* is a major disappointment. In view of the liberal language and the liberal make-up of the SCC, the expectation or hope for a just and fair interpretation of section 35(1) was betrayed. By importing a limitation scheme where none was intended, the SCC has diminished the capacity of section 35(1) to fulfil its promise to the aboriginal peoples of Canada.

# Chapter Four

# After the *Sparrow* Decision

The heady days following the *Sparrow* decision involved a great deal of cheerleading, and there was much speculation on what the decision would mean for the welfare of the aboriginal peoples of Canada. The decision was hailed as an example of how the law can be used to achieve legal and social justice. Within months of the decision, the political science department at the University of Victoria organized a conference to discuss the implications of *Sparrow*. Legal experts, scholars, politicians, aboriginal leaders, supporters and opponents convened to discuss and analyze the decision. Some posited the view that section 35(1) was not an "empty box" but rather a "full box," that the SCC had accorded to the aboriginal peoples everything they wanted, and that the constitution included a full and extensive recognition of aboriginal and treaty rights. Critics of the decision argued that, notwithstanding its apparent constitutional import, *Sparrow* had decided nothing. But there were more supporters than critics, and many got carried away by the rhetoric of the court's decision and engaged in some wildly speculative predictions. Some even argued that the decision meant that aboriginal peoples now had the authority to make laws regulating the use and exchange of fish. There was even talk that *Sparrow* had paved the way to resolving the demands of many First Nations organizations for self-government (University of Victoria 1990).

Legal and theoretical arguments and speculation aside, the questions that need to be addressed, and to this day have not been, are really quite straightforward: What has the *Sparrow* decision meant to the aboriginal peoples of Canada? What has the decision meant to the Musqueam Indian Band that took the case to the Supreme Court? Has the economic situation of this Band improved? Has social transformation occurred? Has it meant access to a valuable natural resource where none had existed before? Has there been a change leading to improvements in accessibility to fish? Are aboriginal fishers now able to exercise their rights without hindrance and/or interference? Has the spirit and intent of the decision been respected or enforced?

To answer these questions, I shall examine the nature of aboriginal fishing rights after the *Sparrow* decision. To provide perspective, it is imperative to also consider the position of the other major players in the fishing industry: the Department of Fisheries and Oceans and the commercial fishing industry. In 1992 the government of Canada, citing its obligations under the *Sparrow* decision, implemented a multimillion-dollar program known as the Aboriginal Fisheries Strategy (AFS), which was promoted by the government as a means to enhance aboriginal participation in the fishing industry. On the other side, the

*Sparrow* decision and the AFS have served as rallying cries for the commercial sector, which has waged an all-out war against the aboriginal fishery. I shall conclude with a review of court challenges that have attempted to build upon the "victory" in *Sparrow*.

## FISHING RIGHTS BEFORE AND AFTER *Sparrow*

As outlined before, aboriginal fisheries have long, rich and varied histories. From their position of reverence to their use as an economic commodity, fish have been, and continue to be, of vital importance to the aboriginal way of life in fishing communities along the coast and inland waters of B.C. and elsewhere in Canada. With the coming of European settlers in the early 1800s, there have been constant and sometimes violent conflicts between whites and aboriginal peoples over fish. Eventually, and with deliberation, aboriginal peoples were legislated out of the lucrative commercial market and were marginalized to an increasingly restrictive regime of fishing for food only. After 1888, aboriginal fishers had no legal right to fish unless accorded so by the government, and the government did not accord any rights except to allow fishing for food under policy provisions. The aboriginal peoples continued to maintain that they had an inherent right to fish, a right that had never been given up, and continued to defy the state through court challenges, "fish-ins" and other forms of protests. In turn they were harassed, intimidated, prosecuted, convicted of criminal offences, fined and/or jailed. And still the aboriginal peoples persisted in claiming their inherent right to fish, a right that had no basis in Canadian law and was not recognized by the government of Canada (Newell 1993; Pearse 1982).

In 1984 the Musqueam Indian Band took a calculated risk and decided to test the promise contained in section 35(1) in the new Canadian constitution. The *Sparrow* decision remains the most significant legal victory in the fight for the recognition of an aboriginal right to fish. The court challenge took several years and cost hundreds of thousands of dollars before the SCC decided that aboriginal peoples had a constitutionally protected right to fish.

Before the decision, aboriginal peoples had no legal right to fish for food or for any other reason. After the decision, they gained a legal right to fish not only for food but to fulfil societal needs and ceremonial purposes. The decision was significant for two major reasons: (1) it was the first time a Canadian court had recognized such a right and (2) it was a huge moral victory for peoples accustomed to losing court battles.

However, any measure of significance, legal or otherwise, is relative and must be tempered with reality. In practical terms, the decision has so far proven insignificant and represents a smoke screen of the highest order, achieved by the obfuscation of legal rhetoric. Furthermore, even the "victory," however slight, has been rendered ineffective and meaningless due to the combined, but not necessarily collusive, efforts of the DFO and commercial interests.

Before the SCC decision, the aboriginal food fishery was allocated 3 percent of the total allowable catch of salmon. The lion's share was held by the commercial fishery at 94 percent, and the remaining 3 percent was held by the sports fishery. In order to allow the aboriginal fishing communities to meet their food requirements, the DFO accorded first priority to the aboriginal fishery, subject only to conservation needs. However, as already indicated, the aboriginal fishers never did enjoy first priority in practice. Frequently, and with regularity, the commercial fishery would catch more than its allocated share, leaving the aboriginal fishery to bear the brunt of any conservation measures. The DFO was aware of this problem and was advised by the Pearse Commission to address the matter but did not do so. In fact the DFO did not even make the attempt, because they were up to something else quite sinister. During the early 1980s, it became common practice for the DFO to depend upon the "shadow" effect to deprive aboriginal fishers of access to the resource. The "shadow" effect is created by the migrating salmon and the corresponding harvest. The salmon move upstream in cycles; if one particular cycle is fished out, it usually takes up to four days for another cycle to move up the river and replace the harvested fish. The delay in the arrival of the next cycle of salmon creates "holes" in the river where there are no migrating salmon. The DFO would allow the commercial fisheries to harvest huge amounts of fish before the salmon entered the river system, and then the DFO would open up fishing to aboriginal fishers, knowing full well that there were no fish to be caught; the aboriginal fishery would be shut down again when the next cycle of salmon started approaching the river system. In other words, the DFO would allow the aboriginal fishers to fish only on days when there were "holes" in the river system, and would feign ignorance when native groups complained that there were no fish to be caught. This trickery stopped only when aboriginal fishers became aware of what the DFO was doing and made it clear that they would not tolerate continued abuses.[5]

For anyone hoping for clarity in the decidedly muddy waters of fishing rights, the SCC decision was a disappointment. The situation after the decision remains unchanged, with one minor exception: aboriginal fishing rights pertaining to food, societal needs and ceremonial purposes are now legally recognized. Nothing else has changed. The subject of fishing rights remains confusing and ill-defined, and the battle over fish continues unabated in the political arena, in the fishing waters and in courthouses across Canada. The conflict between the mostly white commercial fishery and the aboriginal fishery continues and has in some respects intensified. The commercial sector is still allocated 94 percent of the salmon catch and the aboriginal share remains at 3 percent. Most importantly, it is still illegal for an aboriginal person to sell fish caught under the provisions of food fishery.

However, a "before and after" analysis provides only a glimpse of what is happening in the fishing industry in B.C. (and elsewhere in Canada where aboriginal fishers compete for fish stocks with other users). The rules of the game may have been changed by the courts, but that does not mean that those making the decisions are playing by those rules.

## THE GOVERNMENT RESPONSE TO *Sparrow*

When the SCC ruled that Ronald Sparrow was exercising an existing aboriginal right to fish at the time of the alleged offence, there was a nearly collective cry of victory in aboriginal communities across Canada. It was this hard-won recognition that led George Erasmus, the former chief of the Assembly of First Nations to declare *Sparrow* a major victory. Upon sober reflection, it is apparent that Mr. Erasmus reacted hastily. The actual effect of the decision has been, in fact, to limit the aboriginal right to parameters that allow continued state control. The SCC was quite precise: the aboriginal right to fish applies only to food, social and ceremonial purposes, and nothing more.

However, if one is accorded a legal right, even in a manner that actually limits it, that right has to have some meaning or effect. The ideology of law dictates that the legal recognition of a right means a legal protection of that right. It means that a right is to be exercised by the holder without interference and that the holder is to be provided with protection when or while exercising that right. A right is rendered meaningless if one is unable to exercise it. A right is similarly meaningless if one is denied that right or prevented from exercising it.

In according legal recognition to the aboriginal food fishery, the SCC also ordered that aboriginal food fishery be accorded top priority, subject only to the needs of conservation. The SCC stated:

> The significance of giving the aboriginal right to fish food top priority can be described as follows. If, in a given year, conservation needs required a reduction in the number of fish to be caught such that the number equalled the number required for food by the Indians, then all the fish available after conservation would go to the Indians according to the constitutional nature of fishing rights. If, more realistically, there were still fish after the Indian food requirements were met, then the brunt of conservation measures would be borne by . . . sports fishing and commercial fishing (*Sparrow* 1990: 414).

The SCC, as if anticipating future government conduct, was particularly emphatic on the preceding matter and clearly intended the decision to act as a strong check on legislative power. The court stated that any regulation affecting aboriginal food fishing must be justifiable and must meet the test set out above. The court also added that there can be no underlying unconstitutional objective such as shifting more of the resource to a user group that ranks below the priority accorded to the aboriginal food fishery.

However, according to the grand chief of the Sto:lo Nation, Clarence Pennier (1995: A34), and anonymous sources in the DFO, that is exactly what happened in the 1995 fishing season. Even with the weight of the SCC decision, the precise direction of the judges and constitutional protection, aboriginal fishing rights remained subject to almost whimsical and arbitrary control by the DFO, and have yet to be accorded top priority. Aboriginal fishing rights, which are constitutionally protected, continue to be ignored by the government of Canada.

Not only does the aboriginal fishery not receive top priority, but fish that originally had been allocated to aboriginals as a food fishery have been taken away and shifted to other user groups. The fish that the Bands along the coast of British Columbia were not permitted to catch was simply given over to the commercial fishing interests. The action by the DFO, with full support at the ministerial level, was and is illegal, unconstitutional and in complete and blatant violation of the *Sparrow* ruling.

Once again, as at countless times in history, aboriginal fishers have been powerless to change the situation. Some have complained. The Chemainus Tribal Council wrote to the federal minister in charge of fisheries and urged compliance with the *Sparrow* ruling and the AFS agreement. It never received a reply.

One of the fundamental, and perhaps contradictory, problems with winning legal rights is that those who are accorded rights must often fight to protect or exercise those rights. And often that struggle entails taking the matter to the courts. However, most aboriginal Bands lack the resources necessary to fight court cases and, contrary to popular belief (see, for example, British Columbia Fisheries Survival Coalition 1994: 13), are not funded by the state to do so. There are other complicating factors, such as the need to gather evidence, to travel great distances and to take the time required to leave the fishing grounds and attend court miles away. In addition, most Bands have no desire to attend court and only do so as a last resort, and the absurdity of the matter is not lost on the aboriginal fishers. If one court ruling is not obeyed, what assurance is there that subsequent court rulings will be respected? Clearly, there is something fundamentally and morally wrong when a government department deliberately violates its constitutional obligations and its supposed "trust-like" relationship for the sake of political expediency and profits for the multinationals and white fishers.

The effect of such government actions can be devastating. A closure of the aboriginal fishery means more than just a denial of food. It is a denial of a way of life, and the effects have profound implications. The situation worsens further upriver, as one gets to the more remote, isolated and virtually inaccessible villages. What may seem like a simple action (i.e., the closure of fisheries) is anything but a small matter to these remote aboriginal communities. Fishing entails considerable planning; the fisher must travel through inhospitable terrain for days, or arrange for transportation, to synchronize his arrival at the traditional fishing grounds with DFO opening dates. Upon arrival, the fisher is often informed by helicopter or boat patrol that he or she cannot fish. With no food fish to supply their families or other Band members, aboriginal fishers are left to find other sources of food. According to some observers (Ellis 1996; Glavin 1996b) and anonymous DFO officials, remote aboriginal Bands are starving because they have not been allowed to catch food fish. Furthermore, the closure amounts to a denial of an activity that is fundamental to aboriginal culture. The matter does not receive much publicity because the Bands are distant and isolated, and they generally want nothing to do with government officials.

The preceding also holds true for the 1992, 1993 and 1994 seasons. It is not a coincidence that the statistics correspond to the years in which the AFS was in operation. The AFS was supposed to accord to the aboriginal fishing communities more control over fishing and it was supposed to increase aboriginal participation and involvement in the management of fish, but none of this has happened. In fact, the opposite has happened, in a deliberate and insidious manner. In the years since 1992, most of the aboriginal Bands who depend on fish for food have not been able or permitted to catch their pre-season allocations of salmon. Most upriver or interior Bands have caught less than 30–50 percent of the agreed level (Glavin 1995; David Suzuki Foundation 1995; Ellis 1995). The real picture is demonstrated by comparisons between the "food fish" allocations and the actual catch of the various Bands. For example, the 1995 allocation for the Pacheenaht of Vancouver Island was 4,500 pieces of salmon, but the actual catch was zero. For the Sliammon the allocation was 10,000, and the actual catch was zero. For the Klahoose it was 4,000, but, again, the actual catch was zero. The statistics, with minor variations, are relatively the same for other Bands in B.C. The tables below show the statistics for Vancouver Island Bands (Table 1) and the Fraser River Bands (Table 2). Without exception, not one single aboriginal Band caught its allocated amount. The allocations were arrived at following negotiations between the DFO and individual Bands, and the DFO signed agreements saying that the Bands would be able to catch their respective allocated shares.

The Bands did not catch their allocation because they were told not to by the DFO. The DFO persuaded the Bands that an overriding need for conservation existed, and the Bands cooperated. According to a spokesperson for the Musqueam Band, the Band agreed to stop their fishing because they had agreed with the DFO that a conservation need existed (Becker 1996). However, there was no such conservation need. Rather, the DFO, under intense pressure from the commercial lobby, lied to the aboriginal fishers and simply reallocated the aboriginal food fish to the commercial fishery in direct and blatant violation of the Constitution of Canada. The decision to violate aboriginal fishing rights and the terms of the AFS agreement apparently occurred with the full knowledge of then Federal Minister of Fisheries Brian Tobin. According to an anonymous DFO official, Mr. Tobin had been informed by field staff that there were sufficient salmon to meet both the needs of all the aboriginal Bands and conservation

**Table 1:**
Sockeye Salmon Allocations and Catches for Vancouver Island Bands, 1995

| Band/Tribe/Group | Allocation | Actual Catch |
| --- | --- | --- |
| T'Sou-ke | 300 | 0 |
| Becher Bay | 1,300 | 0 |
| Esquimalt | 1,000 | 0 |
| Songhees | 2,100 | 60 |
| Saanich Tribal Fisheries | 10,000 | 1,247 |
| Tseycum | 2,000 | 0 |
| Pacheenaht | 4,500 | 0 |
| Halalt | 3,500 | 0 |
| Mid-Island Tribal Council | 12,000 | 2,731 |
| Nanaimo | 17,000 | 1,700 |
| Nanoose | 4,500 | 1,850 |
| Sechelt | 15,000 | 5,797 |
| Qualicum | 1,000 | 0 |
| Klahoose | 4,000 | 0 |
| Malahat | 1,200 | 0 |
| Cowichan Tribes | 20,000 | 2,500 |
| Sliammon | 10,000 | 0 |
| Chemainus | 14,000 | 3,100 |

Source: Terry Glavin (1995), David Ellis (1995), Clarence Pennier (1995) and the DFO (1995).

**Table 2:**
Sockeye Salmon Allocations and Catches for Fraser River Bands, 1995

| Band/Tribe/Group | Allocation | Actual Catch |
| --- | --- | --- |
| Musqueam; Tsawassen; Burrard | 140,000 | 134,713 |
| Sto:lo; Katzie; Yale | 450,000 | 422,356 |
| NESFA; NNTC* | 110,000 | 92,349 |
| Stl'atl'lmx Nation | 63,000 | 33,522 |
| Shuswap Nation Fisheries | 21,700 | 1,096 |
| Whispering Pines/High Bar | 12,000 | 68 |
| CTC; ALB; TNG* | 100,000 | 26,094 |
| Carrier-Sekani | 55,000 | 11,309 |
| Carrier-Chilcotin | 5,000 | 16 |
| Lheit-Lit'en Nation | 10,000 | 2,080 |

Source: Management Biology Unit/DFO (1995); provided by Glavin (1995) and updated by Ellis (1995).
* NWSFA = Nicola Watershed Stewardship and Fisheries Authority; NNTC = Niaka'pamux Nation Tribal Council; CTC = Cariboo Tribal Council; ALB = Alkali Lake Band; TNG =

requirements. Nevertheless, the aboriginal fisheries were shut down. For this the commercial industry's public relations machinery must be accorded credit, and the government must be condemned for acquiesence to commercial industry's interests.

A right that has been hard fought for and won, and accorded legal protection, is not much of a right if it cannot be exercised when an explicit prohibition exists. Furthermore. a right is violated when it is arbitrarily taken away and accorded to another party. The SCC had ruled that the government cannot do this, but the government did; the court ruled that the government must consult with aboriginal Bands, but the government did not. The court also ruled that aboriginal fishing rights must be accorded top priority and that the needs of other users are secondary, but the government did not listen. The aboriginal fishers cry foul, but they are ignored. Instead, they are criminally charged when they persist in exercising their constitutional rights, as if *Sparrow* never happened (see Platiel 1995: A5; Glavin 1995). In 1995 a total of 110 charges were laid against aboriginal fishers, the highest in recent memory (anonymous source 1995; Glavin 1996b; Ellis 1996). The local media, which had long ago eliminated their "native beat" reporters, do not bother with the real story and focus instead on aboriginal overfishing and poaching. More often than not, the media portray the white commercial fisher in a sympathetic light, painting the picture of a person in danger of losing his or her livelihood because of "Indian" fishing. The "Indian" is always the "bad guy" as the media focuses on the number of aboriginals criminally charged for violations under the *Fisheries Act*. For example, a front-page headline in the *Vancouver Sun* (1995) proclaimed that "Indians 'mishandled' fishing funds." However, a careful reading of the article reveals the true nature of at least part of the "mishandled" funds. The Kwakiutl Band had redirected a portion of the AFS funds to pay the legal bills of a Band member charged for fishing violations.

The evidence strongly indicates that the DFO has not only shirked its obligations under *Sparrow* but also has deliberately circumvented them. According to a senior fisheries manager at the Pacific Region office of the DFO,[6] the department, under the cover provided by the AFS program, has set out to deliberately override the spirit and intent of *Sparrow* and has done so by misleading and blatantly lying to the aboriginal Bands and the Canadian public.

## THE ABORIGINAL FISHERIES STRATEGY

The Aboriginal Fisheries Strategy may have begun as a well-intentioned and sincere effort to respond to *Sparrow* and address the inequities inherent in the way the DFO had managed fisheries (Copes 1996, interview notes), but what the AFS has become is anything but. The evidence is quite convincing that the AFS has served the interests of the DFO, and the interests of the DFO have always been, and continue to be, the well-being and profitability of the commercial fishing industry.

# After the *Sparrow* Decision

The AFS had its inception in 1992 and is a multimillion-dollar program designed to operate over a seven-year period. In a brochure entitled *West Coast Fisheries: Changing Times* (DFO 1993) and in newspaper advertisements, the DFO promoted the AFS as its response to *Sparrow*. The stated purpose of the program was to enhance aboriginal participation in all aspects of the fisheries; the DFO stated that the AFS would ensure that the constitutional rights of aboriginal peoples to fish would be protected. None of this has occurred. It is telling that a stated objective of the AFS is to minimize the disruption of non-aboriginal fisheries.

The AFS was a belated response to *Sparrow*. The SCC forced the DFO to act, and the DFO did so with considerable reluctance. It is worth noting that the DFO has exhibited a remarkable degree of obstinance: it refused to act after the Pearse Commission of 1982; it refused to act when so recommended by its own commission of inquiry; it refused to act after the passage of section 35(1); and it refused to act immediately after the *Sparrow* decision, taking almost two years to formulate a plan of action. When the DFO finally responded to *Sparrow,* it was with a brilliant sleight of hand that has effectively undermined the marginal "victory" of the *Sparrow* case.

The AFS consists of individually negotiated agreements between the DFO and the various Bands. Central to the agreement is the issue of allocation, or the amount of fish the contracting Band will be permitted to catch. The seasonal allocation is agreed upon by both parties after negotiations. For many of the Bands, the request for a certain number of fish reflects both a political statement and legitimate food requirements. Therefore, an arbitrary decision by the DFO to suspend or cancel the terms of negotiated agreements not only denies the Band fish for food, it also represents a political slap in the face and drives home the message of the Band's lack of political power.

The negotiative process does not occur on a level playing field. Even before arriving at the agreement, the DFO takes pains to ensure that it holds all the cards. To do so, the DFO has engaged in intelligence gathering as if the aboriginal peoples are some kind of Cold War enemy. In an internal memorandum dated 25 July 1995 and obtained through the *Access to Information Act,* the operations manager directs a subordinate to gather information and profiles on aboriginal leaders and community groups as if seeking weaknesses to exploit. Specifically, the operation manager wants a

> list of aboriginal organizations, their representatives and band affilia-
> tions, a description of their constituents and influence, speciality
> issues, connections to other groups outside Pacific Region and other
> important points . . . . [T]he list will include not only chiefs, chief
> councillors and representatives, but also aboriginal people who hold
> significant positions of influence or respect in their communities. The
> test of whether to include an individual is to determine whether an

individual might have reason to be in contact with DFO, or whether DFO
. . . might have reason to contact this individual. (DFO 1990)

The manager also directs the subordinate to create a database and share the information with the land claims section. The letter is directed to a DFO employee of aboriginal background who is also requested to use his contacts to supplement the database.

It is more than apparent that the DFO just does not get the message that the aboriginal peoples are not the enemy or some foreign power that should be spied upon. But that is exactly how the aboriginal peoples are treated by the DFO. The AFS contracts that the Bands sign often exceed ten pages in length and contain all sorts of disclaimers and caveats; such is not the case for commercial users. The nature and extent of the contracts reflect paranoia and mistrust on part of the DFO. Furthermore, the terms of the private contracts between the parties (DFO and aboriginal Bands) are made public, and the distribution list includes those who are opposed to aboriginal fisheries, such as the Fisheries Council of B.C. and the B.C. Fisheries Survival Coalition.

Such is the prevailing attitude that it is not surprising the AFS has not benefited those for whom it was intended. In reality the AFS is a sham and a "con job" of the highest order. What the AFS has done is allow the DFO to maintain the control over aboriginal fisheries that the SCC had taken away. According to a senior manager in the DFO, the AFS "buys" back the authority and control that was lost in *Sparrow*. In other words, the AFS maintains the status quo and allows the DFO to continue its activities as if *Sparrow* had never happened. The AFS allows the DFO to shut down aboriginal fisheries and, to quote one anonymous DFO official, "It allows us to charge and convict Indian people." Under the AFS, the only fact that needs to be established for a successful prosecution is that the accused offender violated a signed agreement; if one was to follow the *Sparrow* "test," then it becomes more onerous and difficult, because the Crown has to establish a host of factors, which makes it difficult to convict an aboriginal person who has exercised his or her right to fish.

An anonymous source in the DFO has characterized the AFS as something between a "screw-up" and a "disaster," with no long-term strategy whatsoever; there is no indication where the AFS is headed and the program is running out of funds. But the AFS has bought time for the DFO and allowed it to function as it did before the *Sparrow* decision. This same source, however, credits the AFS for slowing the decline in the rapidly deteriorating relationship between aboriginal fishers and the DFO.

There is no denying that there have been, and continue to be, abuses (i.e., poaching) by all users in the fishing industry. Those who have been most often accused of poaching, the aboriginal fishers, are not the only abusers. However, some observers of the fishing industry, including DFO officials, readily acknowledge that aboriginal Bands have been most cooperative (Glavin 1995,

Ellis 1996). The aboriginal Bands that are signatories to the AFS have fully cooperated with the DFO and have honoured their end of the agreements; not so for the DFO. For example, the AFS agreement signed with the Sto:lo Nation contains a dispute settlement mechanism with clearly and precisely defined conflict resolution directions. When the Sto:lo, aggrieved by a blatant violation of the agreement by the DFO, requested mediation, the DFO refused to participate and proceeded to cut in half the pre-season salmon allocation for the Sto:lo and to reallocate it to the commercial fisheries. According to a DFO official, the department refused to participate because it knew it was in the wrong, the DFO was not prepared to accept any position but its own, and it feared that the ruling would go against it and cause embarrassment. The DFO avoided mediation by falling back on its bag of tricks, arguing that any decision of the mediation panel would encumber the minister of fisheries, and according to administrative principle the minister's prerogative cannot be encumbered.

It is difficult to disagree with some senior DFO officials who state that the AFS has nothing to do with fishing but everything to do with the larger picture of aboriginal rights and land claims issues. This was borne out by the DFO's request that the signatories to the AFS consider the 1994–95 agreements as "partial fulfilment of the federal Crown's responsibility under the treaty." The AFS had been sold to aboriginal communities as the government's response to *Sparrow*, and it has been sold as a program separate from any treaty negotiations. The request by the DFO caught the aboriginal communities by surprise and they protested. Again, the Chemainus Tribal Council wrote to the Prime Minister's Office on August 10, 1994, and again no one listened. The program designed by two former bureaucrats from the Department of Indian Affairs and Northern Development was meant to gauge public reception to ongoing aboriginal land claims negotiations. One may wonder how accurately the reaction will reflect public opinion, given that the agenda has been hijacked by the commercial users. If one were to gauge the reaction in accordance with the response by the commercial industry, then the future for further meaningful negotiations is indeed bleak.

However, for a sham to be perpetuated it must have some degree of legitimacy, and for at least one Band, the Musqueam Indian Band of Vancouver, the AFS has been a qualified success. But that success is completely dependent upon the goodwill of the DFO, and will be for as long as the program remains politically acceptable.

## THE MUSQUEAM INDIAN BAND DEPARTMENT OF FISHERIES

The Musqueam Indian Band has demonstrated in the past that they are not about to sit idly by as the government rides roughshod over their rights. The Musqueam sued the federal government in the *Guerin* case and won a $10 million settlement; the same Band also challenged the DFO and won in *Sparrow*. It is therefore not surprising that the Musqueam have benefited from the decision and the AFS. There is no question that a few aboriginal Bands have benefited economically, but most of the ninety or so Bands along the coast and inland waters of British Columbia have not received any tangible benefits, economic or otherwise. And whatever moderate success is enjoyed by the few Bands does not take away from the fact that the AFS has not worked for the majority of the native groups and that the DFO has undermined and ignored the *Sparrow* ruling.

When asked about the impact of the decision on the Musqueam Band and its fishers, Chief Joe Becker wryly noted that, immediately following the decision, aboriginal peoples were no longer being criminally charged for fishing violations. However this temporary outcome had more to do with the state of utter confusion among DFO enforcement officers than any shift in policy, or goodwill, on the part of the DFO. Mostly based on a misunderstanding and inaccurate interpretation of *Sparrow*, the senior managers at the DFO panicked, and the enforcement officers out in the field did nothing because of an almost complete lack of guidance from the policy-makers (in Glavin 1993; M. Smith 1995).

The AFS agreement between the Musqueam and the DFO has a provision for a pilot sales arrangement (PSA) for salmon. The agreement does not increase the allocation of salmon to the Musqueam but allows for the sale of a portion of the food fish caught by them. While most of the Bands are signatories to the AFS, only four have signed PSA agreements. This agreement by the DFO did not break any new ground. It only recognized a reality and eliminated an activity that was done under cover of darkness; the Musqueam were selling a portion of their fish anyway. The Musqueam Band has prospered; its members no longer have to fear criminal charges for selling their fish; there is a certain immeasurable degree of respectability to the selling of "food" fish, as the fishers no longer have to engage in surreptitious behaviour. It has meant increased employment for Band members, and fewer are receiving social assistance payments. The AFS agreement has allowed the Band to operate its own department of fisheries with the delegated authority to oversee and manage the Band's fish resources. Overall, Chief Becker expressed satisfaction with the AFS agreement and expressed a hope that it would continue. However, there was no such commitment by the government, and the AFS ended in 1997.

When asked about how many salmon are sold by the Musqueam, Chief Becker is silent. His concern is that when the PSA ends, the DFO will reduce the Musqueam allocation to an amount equal to the difference between what the Musqueam catch and sell. His hope is that the PSA will be expanded. Unfortunately for the Musqueam and other aboriginal fishing communities, this hope in all probability will not translate into reality. According to William Duncan (1996), a senior administrative officer at the DFO, the AFS and PSA will not be extended because the issue has become too controversial. The commercial interests, of course, have worked hard to ensure that the AFS does remain controversial.

The benefits that have accrued to the Musqueam are short-term, and there is no guarantee that the AFS or PSA will continue. Any economic or social benefits the Musqueam have gained under the AFS and PSA are illusory in nature because there is a lack of certainty regarding the continuity of the program. If the DFO decides to pull the plug on the program, then the gains made by the Musqueam will vanish. In order to conclude that social transformation has occurred, the changes or improvements must be of a durable, continuing and substantial nature. The changes must also recognize fundamental issues. The issue here is aboriginal fishing rights, and neither the AFS nor PSA recognizes it; the AFS is a negotiated agreement, and the PSA is at the behest of the DFO and does not arise out of a recognition of the history of aboriginal fishing. The PSA is simply a short-term, pragmatic approach that recognizes a limited aspect of reality and brings out into the open a former activity confined to the black market. The fact that a few Bands prosper from the AFS does not mean that those benefits accrue to the general aboriginal community in Canada. Indeed, the evidence strongly indicates that aboriginal Bands have actually suffered under the AFS. As cited in Tables 1 and 2, most Bands have not been permitted to catch their negotiated allocations of salmon.

## REACTION BY THE COMMERCIAL INDUSTRY

While the *Sparrow* case slowly progressed through the lower courts, no one paid any attention to it. It was simply another in a long line of court challenges and did not even merit attention by the commercial industry. All that changed with the British Columbia Court of Appeal decision and the later affirmation of the substance of this decision by the Supreme Court of Canada. Since then the commercial industry has mounted an all-out war against the aboriginal fishery.

Shortly after the SCC decision, Michael Hunter, president of the Fisheries Council of B.C., which represents the major fish-processing companies, wrote to then Minister of Fisheries Bernard Valcourt and urged that no action be taken. The letter is indicative of the fear felt by the commercial industry, which includes the "Big Four" (B.C. Packers, J.S. McMillan, Ocean Fisheries and the Canadian Fishing Company; another key player is Weston Foods, a multinational food conglomerate and parent company of B.C. Packers). Mr. Hunter wrote (1990, emphasis added):

> Although the *Sparrow* case is a landmark case . . . it should have little effect on your management policy or process and, consequently, upon the rights and interests of commercial users. *Nor does it mean that your enforcement efforts aimed at curbing illegal sales of food fish should in any way be diminished.*

Hunter's letter is incorrect and misleading on at least two accounts. He writes of the "rights" of the commercial users when there is no such thing. The only people with a legal right to fish are the aboriginal peoples, and it is a right that the commercial industry conveniently continues to overlook and challenge when confronted. The letter also makes clear a perception shared by many in the commercial sector: that the aboriginal fisher is to be blamed for poaching activities. The B.C. Fisheries Survival Coalition argues that over 90 percent of fish caught under the provisions of "food fish" policy are sold on the black market by aboriginal fishers. It presents no evidence, stating instead that the matter is "common knowledge" (British Columbia Fisheries Survival Coalition 1994: 12).

According to Chief Joe Becker (1995), things did not change much after the *Sparrow* decision. The ball was in the DFO's court and the government took its time to respond. In 1992, when the DFO finally formulated a response by introducing the AFS, it incurred the wrath of the commercial industry and brought to the fore racist sentiments that had been simmering for decades. The Fisheries Council of B.C. was outraged. The president of the council, Michael Hunter, declared, "Everywhere we turn, control is being given to the Indians" (in Glavin 1993: 8). In that year, 1.2 million sockeye salmon went "missing" and the blame was laid squarely on the aboriginal fishers.

Not to be outdone in being affronted was the B.C. Fisheries Survival Coalition, an industry- and union-supported lobby group formed for the sole purpose of protesting and challenging aboriginal fishing rights. In submissions to a parliamentary committee, and in its typically hyperbolic and blatantly inaccurate fashion, the Coalition argued (1994: 9):

> It is not possible to assess the impact of the *Sparrow* decision without being made aware of the aboriginal influence in the academia, government, and the media . . . [the] deliberate misinterpretation [of the decision] resulted in *Sparrow* having a wide-ranging impact far beyond the legitimate scope of the decision.

The coalition placed advertisements in newspapers and told anyone who would listen that the fishing industry was now racially segregated and that the natives had all the rights, and many in the fishing and non-fishing communities listened and gathered in well-orchestrated protests. Typical of the hysteria was an editorial in the *Vancouver Province* (in Glavin 1993: 11): "Since the native fisheries was expanded following court decisions enforced by Ottawa, the salmon available to commercial fishermen have dwindled alarmingly." Never mind that nothing of the sort happened. The aboriginal fishery was not expanded, but that did not stop the media from perpetuating untruths. The theme was picked up by small community newspapers and the spectre of aboriginal fishing rights spread. The non-fishing community of Summerland protested against the AFS on the premise that, if they did not do so, the aboriginal peoples would use *Sparrow* to demand access to timber for a ceremonial right to totem poles. Another newspaper was headlined "Native Fishing causing Health concern," and the fine print accused aboriginal fishermen of fouling the city because some were seen urinating in the streets (in Glavin 1993: 11).

Michael Hunter continues to maintain that if the court hearing the *Sparrow* case had access to all the facts, mainly the commercial industry's view, the case would never have been decided in favour of the Musqueam. He may be right, judging by recent appellate court decisions (to be discussed later). So stunned was the industry by the *Sparrow* decision that they have sworn to never again be caught off guard. The various lobby groups, representing commercial interests, have retained lawyers whose sole function is to track court cases involving aboriginal rights and to intervene in every such case.

By 1995, the fourth year of the AFS, nothing had changed. The commercial industry continued to be outraged and the natives were still being blamed for almost all the ills in the fishing industry. The commercial users have always maintained that *Sparrow* was misinterpreted by the government; their view is that *Sparrow* dealt with the specific issue of Musqueam fishing rights, and any official redress should therefore be restricted to the grievances of the Musqueam and not applied to the general aboriginal population. Michael Hunter appeared before a parliamentary committee and declared that the AFS was a cover to launder the illegal sale of fish (in Hogben 1994: A2). "We're sick and tired of this racially segregated commercial fishery," declared Phil Eidsvik, director of the B.C. Fisheries Survival Coalition (in Crawley 1995c: A1). "It is wrong to give priority to the aboriginal commercial fishery," adds the Pacific Gillnetters Association (in Crawley 1995c: A1). In 1990, lawyer Chris Harvey, representing the Pacific Fishermen's Alliance, an organization that has been condemned as racist, warned white fishermen that a "back to the jungle, free for all" would occur if aboriginal peoples gained control of the fisheries (in Glavin 1993: 8). And again in 1995 Mr. Harvey was back, this time representing a group of independent fishermen in a class-action lawsuit against the DFO, accusing them of encouraging illegal fishing and illegal sales (by aboriginal communities). The lawsuit also alleged that the DFO took fish from the legitimate commercial fishery and allocated it to the (presumably illegal) aboriginal fishery; Harvey also accused the DFO of expanding the priority rights of aboriginal fishers (*Vancouver Sun,* June 7, 1995: 3).

Once again nothing of the sort has happened. There is no evidence to support Harvey's allegations but they do make great headlines. In fact, the very opposite has happened, and the advantage as always has gone to the commercial industry.

The Mike Hunters, Phil Eidsviks and Chris Harveys aside, no one appears more affronted than Mel Smith. Mr. Smith, a lawyer and consultant to the Reform Party, unleashes his wrath on all things aboriginal in a provocatively titled bestseller, *Our Home or Native Land* (1995). Smith ignores the facts and goes for the emotional jugular. He accuses the government of acquiesence to native demands and the DFO of giving away the fish to aboriginal fishers. Not true, but Smith does not let the truth get in the way of his vitriolic attack on the AFS and the DFO. Smith argues that the commercial industry was healthy until the introduction of the AFS in 1992. Smith (1995: 199–225) adds that there is no evidence that aboriginal fishers were ever marginalized, and he concludes that there is no constitutional validity to the aboriginal commercial fishery. Smith is wrong on all counts, but he continues in his diatribe. It is remarkable that a lawyer, and a consultant to a major political party, should be so uninformed about constitutional issues. But since when does a commercial activity require constitutional validity or approval? There is no such requirement. But this fact does not stop Smith from expecting such a requirement of aboriginal fisheries. In fact, such is the extent of his inaccuracies that Mr. Smith arguably could be charged with the criminal offence of spreading hate propaganda.

Why has the AFS excited so much passion and elicited such a vehement attack from the commercial industry? The AFS was never intended to benefit the aboriginal fishers, even though it had been promoted as such. The real objective of the AFS was to protect the commercial fishery. The AFS has not accorded any special benefit or advantage to aboriginal fishers, even though it has been so interpreted by the commercial sector. For this the DFO and the multinational corporations are to be blamed.

Even though the AFS was heavily promoted as the government's response to *Sparrow,* one of its main objectives was to ensure that the commercial industry would continue to earn profits. The DFO, which has long enjoyed a rather cozy relationship with the multinational fishing companies, designed the AFS so that it would cause as little disruption as possible to non-aboriginal fisheries. However, the promotional material led many commercial fishers and union leaders to believe that fish were being given away. Meanwhile, it is business as usual for the multinationals, for whom the AFS has been a boon. The AFS has firmly united the industry, entrenched it in opposition to aboriginal fishers and diverted attention away from the Fisheries Council of B.C. companies' management practices. It is a unity that has been otherwise rare in a fragmented industry—even more remarkable in an industry not known for labour peace (see Millerd and Nicol 1994: 5). According to Eidsvik, opposition to the aboriginal fishery, and the AFS in particular, has united an industry normally at odds and in competition with itself. Eidsvik (1995) marvels at what strength of unity in opposition the issue of aboriginal fishery has engendered; he says he is able to organize protests with "just a few phone calls" (interview notes).

For this the major fish-processing companies are no doubt thankful. The fishing industry is dominated and controlled by the fish processors who had cornered the market long ago and were instrumental in initially marginalizing the aboriginal fisher. The market is dominated by the "Big Four" and the capital-intensive nature of the industry keeps competition to a minimum, although there are several other smaller processors (Pinkerton 1987). The AFS has helped to divert attention away from the oligopolistic nature of the fish-processing market and the firm control that the processors exert upon the industry. The Fisheries Council of B.C., which represents the major processors, has worked hard to keep competition among its members to a minimum and to control the price that the processors pay to the fishers who supply them with the raw resources (Pinkerton 1987: 72–73). According to Ellis (1996), most of the individual commercial fishers (trollers and gillnetters) are not particularly fond of the multinationals because most fishers are financially or otherwise obligated to sell the fish they catch to them. The fishers who have a vested interest in the continued viability and survival of the industry have been led to believe that the aboriginal fisheries, at an insignificant 3 percent of the total allocation, will lead to the destruction of a viable industry and create massive unemployment among the ranks of the white fishers.

The companies have not only exploited the fishers but have also manipulated them in subtle and not-so-subtle ways. For example, some of the processors pay bonuses to the skippers of fishing boats to buy their loyalty; the bonus is not shared with the crew and is not part of the union's collective agreement with the processors. These bonuses undermine union solidarity and create a perception for the skipper that she or he is part of management when in reality the role is essentially a line function (Pinkerton 1987: 76). The processors also assist in financing vessels; they provide accounting and banking services to fishers (Koss 1991:2).

The multinational corporations, primarily the Canadian Fishing Company, B.C. Packers, J.S. McMillan, and Ocean Fisheries, cornered the fishing market long ago. These companies, and major parent company Weston Foods, control almost the entire production and distribution of B.C. salmon products (Pinkerton 1987: 66–89; Glavin 1993: 8). Simon Reisman, a prominent negotiator in the Canada-U.S. free trade talks, sits on the board of directors of a company controlled by Weston Foods, which operates processing plants on both sides of the border (Glavin 1993). These companies have guaranteed themselves the lion's share of the salmon catch in several ways: (1) both Canadian and American fishers supply their processing plants on both sides of the border; (2) these companies or commercial fisheries are allocated 94 percent of the salmon stock by the DFO; (3) because these companies control or own the processing plants, most of the independent commercial fishers have little choice in deciding to whom to sell their catch; (4) the major companies also hold a giant share of commercial fishing licenses; and (5) they own or control the seine fleets, which catch the most salmon (Pinkerton 1987; Muszynski 1987; Glavin 1993).

The outrage exhibited by the multinationals is difficult to fathom in view of the fact that their control over fish is not seriously threatened by anyone, notwithstanding *Sparrow* and other court challenges. The corporate-controlled seine boats comprise 12 percent of the total fishing fleet, which consists of seiners, trollers and gillnetters, yet they catch over 50 percent of the sockeye salmon. Of all the B.C. Fisheries Survival Coalition companies, two corporations, B.C. Packers and the Canadian Fishing Company, own 35 percent of the seine boats (forty-seven and ninety-three respectively) and control most of the fish-processing plants in B.C. In 1993, for example, the total sockeye salmon catch by both B.C. Packers and the Canadian Fishing Company was greater than the combined allocation of salmon to all of the aboriginal communities in B.C. According to the trollers and gillnetters, there is also a constant struggle to hold on to their share of the commercial quota and to prevent all of the fish from being caught by the corporate seine boats. Even then it is a losing battle. Most of the individual fishers have very limited options when it comes to selling their catch—the only buyers are the Fisheries Council of B.C. companies, which often purchase the fish at artificially low prices. David Ellis has characterized the relationship between the individual commercial fisher and the corporate sector as "feudal." The companies have baited and used these fishers in their battle against aboriginal fishing (Howard 1996: D3; Glavin 1996c: 15; Alden 1996: A19; Ellis 1996).

The exploitation of labour and the constant search for cheaper labour is consistent with the history of fish processing in B.C., and this, of course, runs counter to the objectives of the labour unions (Muszynski 1987: 270–90). Largely built by cheap labour, be it aboriginal, Chinese or Japanese (before the Second World War), the industry has always sought cheap and available labour in the never-ending pursuit of even greater profits for owners and shareholders, the majority of whom have never set foot on a fishing boat. The processors had long ago started shutting plants and eliminating jobs in B.C. In the late 1980s they moved with the tide of the Free Trade Agreement (FTA) opening processing plants in Washington and Alaska and staffing them with lower-paid, non-union labour. They also started shipping B.C. fish to the U.S. for processing. Washington State, for example, is completely dependent upon the export of unprocessed fish from B.C. All this occurs despite provincial legislation, which restricts export of unprocessed fish and other natural resources. Inexplicably, the FTA allows this[7;] however, the apparent exemption applies only to unprocessed fish and not to any other natural resources (Millerd and Nicol 1994: 3). Perhaps there is a connection, given that the chief Canadian negotiator in the free trade talks has some financial interest in the well-being of Weston Foods. B.C. Packers, a subsidiary of Weston, was among the first to open a plant in Washington (Glavin 1993: 11).

Herein lies the greatest threat to unionized and non-unionized labour in the B.C. commercial fishing industry. Instead of uniting to battle against the multinationals, the ordinary fishers are so consumed with opposition to the aboriginal fisheries—with a fervour never seen before—that they have entirely missed the real threat to their livelihood. The export of unprocessed fish has profound implications for workers in the industry, because the number of jobs in the processing operations has steadily declined. From 1974 to 1994, the number of large fish-processing plants in B.C. declined by more than 50 percent in spite of the fact that canned salmon production increased over the same period. Meanwhile, the amount of salmon processed in unionized plants in B.C. continues to fall. Interestingly enough, the Canadian processors on this side of the border are in direct competition with Canadian processors based in the U.S.; the plants are being supplied by both American and Canadian fishers (Millerd and Nicol 1994: 5). It is noteworthy that B.C. Packers of B.C. "competes" with B.C. Packers of the U.S., and it is not difficult to conclude who ultimately profits. It is certainly not the ordinary commercial fisher or plant worker.

When asked to comment, Phil Eidsvik (1995), arguably the loudest opponent, dismisses the suggestion as "conspiracy hogwash" and falls back on his tested rhetoric of "racial segregation" and "everyone should be equal in law." According to the B.C. Fisheries Survival Coalition (1994: 16), the processors are investing outside the country because of the AFS; furthermore the AFS has been labelled as the biggest single destabilizing factor in the industry. The Survival Coalition, the unions and the white fishers have not yet realized that the greatest threat to their livelihood are the multinationals, not aboriginal fishers. However, they are too busy fighting aboriginal fisheries to appreciate their own rather tenuous situation.

The big winners in the war against the AFS and aboriginal fisheries are the companies of the Fisheries Council of B.C. who, having worked hard at limiting competition and ensuring themselves of a dependable supply, are not about to let aboriginal fishers disrupt that. The spectre of aboriginal fishing clearly threatens the industry. But industry members have managed to turn the tables and have used the issue of aboriginal fisheries to protect themselves by portraying themselves both as victims and as the protector of the fish: the supply of fish is limited and rapidly dwindling, and the last thing the companies need is more competition. That is why they have mounted such a vehement assault on aboriginal fishing. So effective has been the campaign that any talk of aboriginal fisheries in non-aboriginal communities elicits fears of ecological and environmental disaster, overfishing and poaching by aboriginal fishers and white fishers being driven to the brink of unemployment.

There is no question that the attack is fuelled by misinformation, fear-mongering and blatant lies—the rhetoric of the attack on the aboriginal fishery has far outstripped the facts. For example, Mike Hunter was queried on why the question of from whom they buy their fish makes any difference to the Fisheries Council of B.C.. According to Hunter (1995), fish caught in the river system are of lesser quality than fish caught in the ocean. Although processors may prefer ocean-caught fish for their quality, the reality is that this provides an excuse not to purchase fish from aboriginal fishers. In fact, the processors can most of the fish and quality is not of primary concern—quantity is (Pinkerton 1987: 73). (The multinational corporations are also constrained by complex labour agreements that stipulate from whom fish are to be purchased.)

The greatest fear of the multinationals can be found in the hopes, dreams and aspirations of impoverished aboriginal communities. These communities hope to create sustainable economic activity to create badly needed jobs where unemployment often reaches 90 percent; in hinterland economies and urban reservations, fish is the one great hope, because currently there is nothing else aboriginal communities can build on to battle the chronic social ills that pervade them all across Canada. However, these hopes also represent an intolerable competition to the multinationals. Having worked at capturing the aboriginal labour in the 1800s, creating a relationship of subordination and dependence, and eventually marginalizing the aboriginal fisher, the commercial processors now fear that aboriginal communities will start cottage industries to process their own fish, in direct competition with them. A hint of what is to come is found in recent negotiations with the Nisga'a in British Columbia, which set in motion the public relations machinery of the commercial industry. Once again the B.C. Fisheries Survival Coalition, the unions and the Fisheries Council of B.C. were all outraged and threatened to sue; they threatened to hound politicians and promised to work at defeating any elected politician opposed to their views. Why? After over twenty years of negotiations, the Nisga'a and the federal and provincial governments are close to an agreement that includes a provision for a Nisga'a-managed fishery on their lands. Under pressure from the commercial lobby, the B.C. government, facing an election, backed away from the agreement, even though it was arrived at after over twenty years of negotiations and has the support of the Nisga'a, the federal government and even a sports fishery organization. This settlement also has the support of several experts in the field, including Peter Pearse and Peter Larkin; the David Suzuki Foundation (1995) described the agreement as "fair, just and reasonable." However, it is the avowed intent of the B.C. Fisheries Survival Coalition and the Fisheries Council of B.C. to scuttle the deal. Hunter, speaking for the council, but speaking as though his position reflects the mood of the general populace, states: "I don't think the public will buy that" (in *Vancouver Sun,* February 2, 1996: B2). Hunter further declared that the agreement will "destroy the fish [and] the industry" (in *Vancouver Province,* February 18, 1996: A30). It is interesting to observe the Fisheries Council's habit of reframing issues of direct interest to them as public issues. Altruism is the last thing with which the commercial industry could be credited. Its only motive is profit. According to a spokesperson for the David Suzuki Foundation, one of the reasons that the commercial industry is opposed to the deal is greed; the industry hoped to realize the profits from the large salmon runs predicted for the 1997, 1998 and 1999 seasons, and they have no intention of sharing the resource (Hume 1996b: B1).

There is no direct evidence that the DFO and the multinationals operate as anything but independent entities, but consider the following points. The DFO has, in the past, participated in executive-exchange programs with the major fishing corporations (Ellis 1996). According to an anonymous source in the DFO, senior DFO officials have gone on all-expenses-paid fishing expeditions with the head of the Sport Fishing Association. The DFO consults with advisory committees, which are essentially an "old boy's network"; these advisory committees, some of which are partially funded with grants from the DFO, consist of prominent people in the industry, including Michael Hunter and others from the commercial industry. Of course, there is also a "token" aboriginal person. From these facts, it is difficult to infer that policy-making at the DFO is entirely free of bias and that it does not favour the companies. However, the DFO is not entirely to blame. The multinationals are powerful entities that employ thousands of workers; whatever actions they take often have profound social and economic implications. According to Marchak (1987: 12), "The power of large corporations necessarily affects and structurally constrains the choices government makes."

The example from 1992, the case of the "missing" fish, illustrates this well. In an award-winning article, Terry Glavin (1993) explains what really happened in 1992. In the weeks preceding the 1992 salmon season opening, the gillnetters, trollers and other small independent fishers eagerly awaited the arrival of the migrating salmon. However, they and the aboriginal fishers were told not to go fishing because 1.2 million salmon had somehow gone missing. The Fisheries Council of B.C. announced that the aboriginal poachers had caught them all. This was blatantly false because the fish had been caught out in the ocean by Fisheries Council companies. The fish that the aboriginal fishers were accused of poaching had been caught by the seine fleets, but that did not stop the Fisheries Council from launching a vehement attack on aboriginal fisheries. Mel Smith wrote a chapter on the matter and accused the aboriginal fishers of stealing the fish. The council went to the Supreme Court of British Columbia seeking an order to stop the just-signed AFS agreements between the DFO and the Lower Fraser Bands; in signed affidavits and evidence gathered by the council's private investigators, the court was told that the fishing industry was facing an ecological disaster and that 1.2 million salmon had been poached by aboriginal fishers. The judge hearing the case dismissed it; Dr. Peter Pearse was hired by the DFO to investigate, but he found no evidence that wide-scale poaching by aboriginal fishers has caused the "disappearance" of the salmon. But the allegations made the headlines and created an uproar (in Glavin 1993: 9; M. Smith 1995).

The commercial industry, particularly the B.C. Fisheries Survival Coalition and the Fisheries Council of B.C., have done a masterful public relations job. The commercial users have effectively portrayed themselves as victims and they explode into outrage at the slightest pretext. There is a great deal of irony in the rallying cry of the white fishers—they cry racism and inequality, while blissfully ignoring the plight of aboriginal fishers, who have rarely been treated as equal in Canadian society. Why, they ask, are "Indians" being given special treatment?

All this occurs while the major fishing corporations continue to make millions of dollars plundering the resource in pursuit of even greater wealth for their shareholders. While such an objective is inherent in a free-market capitalist system, no one takes responsibility for the dwindling stocks. Hypocritically blaming the aboriginal fisher for the ills of the industry diverts attention away from the fundamental causes, which are overfishing and greed on the part of the commercial sector. It is also racism, pure and simple.

There is no mistaking the racist overtones in the hysteria that pervades the fishing industry. This hysteria has been created and perpetuated by the B.C. Fisheries Council companies, the DFO, politicians and white fishers. The public is led to believe that salmon stocks are being plundered by aboriginal fisheries, and that the aboriginals have their own protected commercial industry and all of the advantages because of their race. The reality is often ignored: aboriginal fishers are generally an impoverished lot. A few have been remarkably success-ful, but not because of any special treatment or rights; these are aboriginal fishers who hold licenses and operate as commercial fishers on an equal footing with white fishers. However, they remain the exception rather than the rule. Aboriginal fishers are still confined to the margins of the industry and, in spite of recent court decisions, including *Sparrow*, they remain subject to arbitrary control by the DFO.

A cynic may conclude that such hysteria, animosity, anger, misinforma-tion, lies and vehemence is exactly what the Fisheries Council of B.C. and the DFO want. The issue has become so convoluted and conflated that it has become politically palatable *not* to negotiate fisheries with the Bands; it has become politically palatable *not* to uphold the Supreme Court of Canada decision in *Sparrow*.

## FUTURE (AND CONTINUING) COURT CHALLENGES
The most crucial issue for all te players in the fishing industry boils down to one question. Do aboriginal fishing rights include the right to sell fish for economic or livelihood purposes? The ultimate prize, the right to sell their fish, still eludes aboriginal fishers. Even though the "victory" in *Sparrow* has been rendered almost hollow by the DFO and the commercial industry, the hopes this victory engendered led to several court challenges that attempted to expand upon the rights enunciated in *Sparrow*. Here I shall discuss cases dealing with the commercialization of the rights fishery. *Rights fishery* refers to fish caught as a matter of constitutional right, is limited to "food fish" and does not include fish caught by aboriginal fishers holding commercial licenses.

Aboriginal communities have always maintained that they should be permitted to do with fish whatever best suits their needs, including selling their catch. The commercial industry vehemently disagrees with this position and it was their turn to celebrate when the British Columbia Court of Appeal ruled on the issue of sale. Court challenges initiated by aboriginal communities that argued for a right to sell fish have to date not succeeded. In three major court decisions, the BCCA ruled against the aboriginal right to sell fish. *R.* v. *N.T.C. Smokehouse, R.* v. *Gladstone* and *R.* v. *Vanderpeet* had similar fact situations— in each case an aboriginal person was charged with the offence of selling fish, in each case the defence asserted that the sale occurred under an aboriginal right, and in each case the courts rejected that argument.

Of the three fishing cases, the most important was the *Vanderpeet* decision. While an analysis of this decision is beyond the scope of this study, it does merit some consideration here. Buoyed by the unexpected success of *Sparrow*, the Sto:lo Nation, which had not initially supported the Musqueam's court challenge, decided to test the mettle of what appeared at first glance to be very positive language from the BCCA. The Sto:lo decided to push for an aboriginal right to sell their fish. In spite of anthropological evidence that the Sto:lo had engaged in barter and trade, the BCCA concluded that the Sto:lo had no such right. The court's reasoning resonates with Eurocentric biases. The majority of the court concluded that the Sto:lo had engaged in barter and trade of fish but characterized the activity as incidental and informal. The court maintained that commercial activity was created by the arrival of the Hudson's Bay Company's trading posts, precluding the possibility that the Sto:lo possessed the business acumen to exploit or develop new markets for their fish. Don Ryan, a spokesperson for the Gitksan Wet'suwet'en remarked, "We got hammered. This has pushed us back to the high water mark" (in J. Smith 1995: 220).

All of the preceding cases, *Vanderpeet, Gladstone* and *N.T.C Smokehouse,* were appealed to the Supreme Court of Canada. I discuss the outcome of the appeals in the Postscript, which follows the conclusion of this book.

## CONCLUSION

In answering the questions posed at the beginning of this chapter, it is difficult not to conclude that the DFO, and the government, has violated the spirit and intent of the SCC decision in *Sparrow*. The hope that arose out of *Sparrow* led many to speculate that it would mean aboriginal access to a valuable resource, but this has not happened. There was a hope that aboriginal fishers would be able to exercise their guaranteed constitutional rights without hindrance or interference, but this has not happened. While some First Nations have benefited, most have not.

The outcomes in the wake of *Sparrow* raise doubts about whether rights litigation is an effective strategy for the disadvantaged to achieve social transformation.

# Chapter Five

# *Sparrow,* the Law
# and Social Transformation

The 1995 fishing season was not a good season for the aboriginal fisher, nor was it a particularly productive year for commercial fishers (J. Smith 1995; Cernetig 1996; Crawley 1995b: A1). Just before the August 1995 opening date for aboriginal-only fishing at the mouth of the Fraser River, Ernie Crey, executive director of the Sto:lo Nation Fisheries Authority, was interviewed on a local newscast and asked to comment on the threats by the B.C. Fisheries Survival Coalition to disrupt the opening (see *Vancouver Sun,* August 8, 1996: A1). Mr. Crey replied that it would be best for the Survival Coalition to reacquaint itself with the law, because the aboriginal fishers would be exercising their constitutional rights to fish (in accordance with the SCC decision in *Sparrow* and section 35(1) of the *Constitution Act, 1982*). To a query regarding appropriate government response if the Survival Coalition made good on its threats, Crey replied "presumably they will be arrested" (Canadian Broadcasting Corporation [CBC] 1995; see also Crawley 1995c: B2).

Opening day came and the Survival Coalition, as they had threatened, disrupted the fishing. The televised scenes of mayhem in the waters of the Fraser River resounded with celebratory yells by the white fishers as their boats churned up the waves around the aboriginal fishing boats. The police and DFO officials stood by and no one was arrested or charged. No one, that is, except John Cummins, MP for the Reform Party, who insisted upon being arrested and charged to publicly demonstrate his objection to the aboriginal-only fishing. Mr. Cummins, a former fisher, has continually spearheaded protests and publicity campaigns against aboriginal fishing rights; his tactics receive considerable media coverage. He continues to maintain that aboriginal fishers are being "greedy" in their demands for fish.

As one Survival Coalition member put it (in J. Smith 1995: A5), "Why should they get to fish first . . . it's not fair." In their zealous attempts to thwart aboriginal fishing and gain publicity, the coalition deliberately overlooked some obvious facts: aboriginal food fishing is constitutionally guaranteed, and the aboriginal opening was only for twelve hours on a day when the tides were running out (fish do not swim to spawning grounds when the tides are out), while the commercial fleet was scheduled for a twenty-four-hour opening the next day (Mearns 1995). And even in that twelve-hour opening, there was no way the aboriginal fishers would have been able to catch their allocation. The Sto:lo Nation threatened to sue the DFO and demanded that they be allowed to fish for a longer period, but to no avail (in J. Smith 1995: A5).

In addition to legitimate democratic protests, the B.C. Fisheries Survival Coalition has also engaged in publicity stunts (e.g., wrapping the Pacific Region DFO office in Vancouver with fishing nets) and in the harassment of aboriginal fishers and the destruction of their property. For the coalition, the battle is personal and motivated by malice and a genuine, if misguided, concern about the state of the industry. During the course of an interview, Phil Eidsvik (1995), spokesperson for the coalition, handed me an eight-by-ten photograph of Ron Sparrow's large, sprawling residence and rhetorically asked, "Does he look like he needs more fish?" Terry Glavin (1996b) reports that harassment of aboriginal fishers by coalition members occurs frequently; in one incident a member of the Tsawassen Band, who was returning from fishing, was prevented from docking for almost two hours; when he finally was allowed to dock, he found that all four tires in his vehicle had been slashed. During the August 1995 protests, Musqueam fishers lost some of their nets and came close to having their boats "swamped" as Survival Coalition boats circled the smaller aboriginal boats (Becker 1996).

In his 1996 annual report, Max Yalden, head of the Human Rights Commission of Canada declared, once again, as he has for the past nine years, that the most pressing human rights problem facing Canada is the plight of its First Peoples. The successes associated with mainstream Canadian society continue to elude the aboriginal peoples dispersed across Canada; an over-whelming number of aboriginal peoples live in third world conditions in one of the most affluent nations in the world.

During the nine years in question, and indeed since the dawn of white settlement in Canada, the aboriginal peoples have not been passive recipients of all that successive governments have meted out. Aboriginal peoples have fought and continue to fight for a foothold in Canadian society; for political, social, legal and economic equality; to be heard, to be recognized, and to be treated as equals in a society that has, by both subtle and blatant means, relegated them to the margins. In spite of all that has occurred, aboriginal peoples continue to survive in Canada. And that achievement in and of itself is quite remarkable in face of the many attempts to destroy, subdue, control and subjugate them. Furthermore, the natural resources of which the aboriginal peoples were once the only users and guardians continue to be expropriated and exploited without compensation. When the resources being expropriated are on lands under treaty negotiations, the expropriation has been accelerated by companies eager to get as much wealth from the resources as possible before the lands are "won" under land claims agreements by aboriginal groups. This problem has become so severe that the B.C. Treaty Commission filed a complaint with the provincial government (O'Neil 1996a: A1).

In attempts to protect their rights, aboriginal peoples have engaged in a variety of actions ranging from peaceful to violent. Aboriginal peoples have blockaded roadways and railways; occupied DFO offices; deliberately defied

DFO orders; ignored DFO directives to obtain fishing licenses; filed lawsuits and sought court injunctions against government and private interests that infringe upon their rights; and engaged in violent and armed confrontation with the state. As documented by Newell (1993), the aboriginal peoples of Canada have never given up what they view as their inherent right to fish or hunt; they have continually fought for a legal recognition of a right to do with the fish what their ancestors have done from time immemorial, without requiring the permission of the state. In recent years an increasing number of aboriginal tribes and Bands have been turning to the law to advance their causes and protect their rights. These attempts provide insight into the efficacy of the oft-claimed transformative capacity of law. As evidenced by the preceding case study of a "landmark" Supreme Court of Canada decision dealing with aboriginal rights, this strategy is fraught with pitfalls.

## LAW AND SOCIAL TRANSFORMATION

For the disadvantaged in liberal-democratic societies, a largely untested hypothesis has been that the law can be used as means of social transformation. The theoretical suppositions that have given rise to the whole debate about the efficacy of law as a tool for social transformation are remarkably lacking in substantive evidence and are based on the premise that winning legal battles results in social progress. Many proponents cite the supposed successes of the women's movement and the American civil rights movement to support their arguments in favour of legal attempts by subordinate classes to further objectives of social, economic and/or political equality (Brickey and Comack 1989; Fudge 1990). However, a closer and critical examination of the gains made by the preceding movements indicates a complex variety of factors at play that can hardly be reduced, or ascribed, to the law as being the causal factor.

Let us take, for example, the issue of abortion and the ongoing battle between the two polarized groups, pro-life and pro-choice. The pro-choice movement has fought a long and still continuing battle for freedom of choice, arguing that the question of abortion is solely for the person considering it. The pro-life movement, a bastion of conservative and religious values, has argued otherwise and has, until recently, prevailed in law (insofar as abortions had to be approved by a hospital committee). When the SCC decided the *Morgentaler* case, there was a collective cry of victory from various women's rights organizations—a response similar to that elicited by the *Sparrow* decision. And like the *Sparrow* decision, there was much debate and learned commentary regarding *Morgentaler*. Like *Sparrow,* the *Morgentaler* decision resonated with high-sounding moralistic rhetoric (see, for example, the reasons stated by Justice Bertha Wilson). However, what the celebrants and many learned commentators overlooked was the fact that the SCC did not legalize abortion or accord women an unrestricted right, or any right, to abortion. The court simply ruled that the procedure in place, requiring the approval of a hospital committee, was too onerous and therefore a violation of constitutional rights. The SCC clearly left the door open for future legislative action aimed at controlling or criminalizing abortion. There are no guarantees and, more importantly, there is no protection against future legislative action.

The same holds true for aboriginal rights. The SCC, in *Sparrow,* imported into its analysis of section 35(1) an interpretative procedure that has had the effect of actually limiting the scope of rights originally envisioned by aboriginal organizations. The decision paves the way for future courts to limit and control aboriginal rights. More importantly, the decision provides the state with the legal justification to control aboriginal rights. The state has the means to legitimize regulatory control, contrary to what section 35(1) guaranteed.

With nothing but theoretical suppositions to support it, the *Morgentaler* case has often been held up as an example of the transformative capacity of law (see analysis by Fudge 1990). What such arguments clearly overlook are the decades of political lobbying and other factors (protests, shifts in paradigm, changes or advancements in economic status, empowerment, etc.) that have contributed to social progress. It is problematic indeed to ascribe to the law successes in an arena where it is distinguished by a conspicuous lack of success. On this point, Justice Gerard LaForest is succinct (in *R.* v. *Andrews* 1990: 38):

> Much economic and social policy making is simply beyond the institutional competence of the courts. Their role is to protect against incursions on fundamental values, not to second guess policy decisions.

While that may be true of the role of the courts, the law encompasses a broader field. However it is left up to the courts to interpret legislation, and even when such legislation has had the announced intention of ameliorating social ills, the courts have fallen short, as evidenced by, for example, the Supreme Court's interpretation of section 35(1). Therein lies perhaps the most fundamental of problems, that of burdening an institution of redress with issues that have immense social implications that it is not suited to consider. It is important to recognize the shortcomings of this strategy, notwithstanding its conceivable promises. Indeed, there is considerable evidence that law, as a tool for social transformation, lacks efficacy (see, for example, litigation under the Canadian *Charter of Rights and Freedoms* in Mandel 1989 and 1996; Fine 1995; McCormick 1993). Why is there so much faith in law? Ideology offers an explanation, and one need look no further than the ultimate ideological weapon, the *Charter,* which declares in section 15:

> Every individual is equal before and under the law and has the right to equal protection and benefit of the law without discrimination and, in particular, without discrimination based on race, national or ethnic

origin, colour, religion, sex, age or mental or physical ability.

In his unrelenting and scathing criticism of the *Charter*, law professor Michael Mandel (1989: 240), makes the following observation: "It is no accident that the *Charter* list of items according to which we must be equal in law are the very things according to which we are unequal in life." Mandel's point is well taken. Legal rights do not recognize the realities of economic, political and social relations of domination and subordination.

When it comes to issues of formal equality, the courts have not hesitated. However equality is a political concept and, as always, is relative and rather slippery. It is worth noting that all people, including aboriginal peoples, are formally equal before and under the law, because conferring formal equality does not entail considerable expense to the state, and it does have a lofty moralistic and rhetorical ring to it. Indeed, wealthy corporations have portrayed themselves as individuals and won rights that constitutionally were never intended to serve the interests of non-person entities (see, for example, the legal victory by tobacco companies upholding their right to free speech, to advertise cancer-causing products, contrary to the now unconstitutional legislation banning such activities). Issues of profound economic disparity, unemployment, poverty and other social ills are not redressed by the granting of formal equality, and it is precisely these factors that are arguably the greatest threat to social justice and equality (Mandel 1989).

There are complex reasons why *Sparrow* has failed the aboriginal peoples, and perhaps one should first consider the theoretical supposition itself. Curiously, the hypothesis that winning legal battles leads to social transformation has found acceptance in academic circles without a detailed examination of the evidence. In fact, there is a remarkable lack of evidence in support of this hypothesis and considerable evidence to the contrary. The debate concerning law and social transformation may encourage stimulating intellectual discourse, but it does nothing for subordinate groups still struggling for a foothold in mainstream society. Indeed, a recent survey (Bindman 1996) concluded that trust in the legal system increases with level of income. For example, 46 percent of persons earning under $30,000 per annum said they did not trust the courts; however, 75 percent of those earning over $60,000 trusted the courts. In other words, the higher the income, the higher the trust in the court system. While dominant groups have devised sophisticated means of keeping others out, it seems contradictory to expect that these groups would then allow access to those being kept out. Furthermore, the tool that dominant groups have so successfully manipulated, the law, is also a tool by which the status quo is maintained and perpetuated. An examination of aboriginal fishing rights and the aboriginal peoples' fight for those rights reveals the apparent folly of litigating to advance social causes. As outlined in preceding chapters, it was the government and private companies that drafted the laws that took away those rights in the first place.

## *Sparrow,* the Law and Social Transformation

However, the ideological hegemony of law disguises reality and leads us to believe that the law is a guarantor of justice and equality. But such beliefs overlook a crucial problem and a glaring contradiction: the law often does not act in an evenhanded fashion. How can one be equal in law while being unequal in every other material measurement? And if one is an aboriginal person, then one is especially not equal before the law. The supposedly blinDFOlded symbol of justice has peeked out from under her blinDFOld and acts to perpetuate and legitimate inequality when the person standing before her is an aboriginal person (Nova Scotia 1989; Manitoba 1991).

Yet faith in law as being capable of redressing gross inequities and evening the odds between subordinate and dominant classes persists in spite of considerable evidence to the contrary (see Fine 1995: A1; Mandel 1996). This faith also extends to the Royal Commission on Aboriginal Peoples, which, in spite of the ruling in *Sparrow,* erroneously contends that section 35(1) allows aboriginal communities the right to interpret and try Canadian laws (see *Globe and Mail* 1996: A20).

This faith, not surprisingly, also extends to those who practice and teach law. According to law professor Kathleen Mahoney (in Fine 1995: A17): "The courts get right into the messy reality of life to decide the very difficult questions of equality and competing rights. I think we are going down the road to real equality." Taking a more sober and reflective view is political scientist Peter Russell, who states (in Fine 1995: A17), "Law professors really love those cases, but that doesn't change the country very much." Professor Peter McCormick (1993) examined all of the Supreme Court of Canada decisions since 1949, the year in which the court became the highest court of appeal in Canada, and concluded that the state and corporations were the major victors in the majority of cases. According to Wood (in Fudge 1990: 50):

> It is precisely the recourse that subordinate groups have had to judicial and political institutions in their relations with the dominant classes, together with restrictions on the "freedom" of the state itself, that have created a faith—though hardly unlimited—in the efficacy of legal and political forms.

Perhaps this is why aboriginal peoples continue to turn to the courts in their struggle for equality and social progress. However, the courts, with remarkable naïveté, tell aboriginal peoples that the courts are not the proper forum and suggest negotiations with the government. The government, in turn, exhibits a reluctance to negotiate and, when negotiations are carried out, it is often lacking in good faith. Aboriginal leaders, frustrated by the slow pace of official negotiations, threaten court action and the cycle continues. Don Ryan, spokesperson for the Gitksan and Wet'suwet'en, readily acknowledges the shortcomings of both forums, stating that they have been frustrated at every turn by both the government and the courts, but he nevertheless vows to continue the legal battle (in Simpson 1993: A9). Philip Joe, of the Squamish Nation, is clearer still of his position, threatening to take his fight to the courts if negotiations fail (Noble 1996: 3).

The major problem with such an approach is that when one plays by the rules set out by the dominant classes, one cannot expect much more than a symbolic victory. In the final analysis, that is exactly what *Sparrow* was, and nothing more. However, in their fight for legal rights, and for fish, aboriginal peoples are not going to be satisfied with symbolic victories. *Sparrow* was more than a demand for a symbolic victory and more than a demand for formal legal rights. It was and is a challenge to the Canadian state, and a direct challenge to the multinationals that dominate and control the fishing industry in British Columbia.

However, the commercial industry has not taken kindly to this challenge and has fought back, and the battle has become bitter and vicious. Although the two major combatants (aboriginal peoples and multinational corporations) are assumed to be on an equal footing in the courts and are guaranteed equality before the law, the reality is otherwise. A fundamental problem with court battles is that they disguise the enormous imbalances in power and resources, because these two parties are anything but equal. And as evidenced by the government response to *Sparrow,* the multinational corporations have won the battle for fish. This outcome is not surprising, for it was never a fair fight to begin with.

## WHY HAS *Sparrow* FAILED TO DELIVER?

> The *Sparrow* decision is a . . . tool that aboriginal communities can use to advance their cause (Isaac 1991: 379).

In both legal and practical terms, *Sparrow* has not served the interests of the aboriginal peoples. It has failed aboriginal peoples in two significant ways: the legal decision itself has failed them and so has the state's response. In reviewing *Sparrow,* it is puzzling that it should be called a "landmark" decision. "Landmark" for whom? As outlined in Chapter Four, the decision has not altered to any great degree the aboriginal peoples' fight for fish or the status of fishing rights. The most fundamental issue (concerning the right to sell) remains unresolved. The decision has not accorded any advantage to the aboriginal fisher. Aboriginal fishing rights and aboriginal access to a valuable natural resource remain subject to arbitrary and almost whimsical control by the DFO, even though this control is now exercised in a more sophisticated manner. The courts continue to pay lip service but offer little in the way of substantial redress. Nowhere is this better illustrated than in two recent decisions by the Supreme Court of Canada in *R.* v. *Nikal* and, to a lesser degree, *R.* v. *Lewis.* Interestingly enough, both aboriginal leaders and the commercial industry proclaimed these two decisions as a victory for them (for obviously different reasons) (Bell 1996: A1).

Jerry Benjamin Nikal was caught fishing for salmon in the Bulkley River which flows through his reserve. Mr. Nikal was on reserve property and maintained that the requirement to obtain a fishing license was an infringement of his constitutional rights. Nikal further maintained that only his Band could regulate fishing on reserve property. Nikal was acquitted at trial and also upon further appeal by the Crown. The B.C. Court of Appeal reversed the findings of the two lower courts and found Mr. Nikal guilty, and the finding was upheld by the SCC upon appeal by Nikal.

On the one hand the commercial industry declared the *Nikal* decision as a victory for conservation, even though the manner in which they have plundered, exploited and wasted the resource hardly qualifies them as advocates of conservation. However, this is entirely in keeping with the image that the companies hope to project, given that they have accused the aboriginal fishers of widespread poaching and decimation of salmon stocks. On the other hand, aboriginal leaders, grasping at apparent straws, also declared *Nikal* a victory, and this was based on an issue already decided by the courts in *Sparrow.* In *Nikal* the SCC rejected the aboriginal argument that they controlled the rivers running through reserve property (a flawed argument to begin with, given that reserve land is legally Crown land, not aboriginal land), stating that the Bands had no right to regulate fishing in those waters. The SCC also ruled that aboriginal fishers must obtain licenses from the DFO in order to exercise their rights to fish. It is interesting to note the comments of Justice Millward of the Supreme Court of British Columbia when he examined the licensing requirement. Millward concluded that the food fish licensing infringed Mr. Nikal's aboriginal right and he rejected the DFO's position that licensing was an important control feature meant to safeguard the fish stock. Justice Millward stated that conservation measures should be directed first at other users because aboriginal fishers were to be accorded top priority; Millward also noted that the licensing scheme achieves little and merely provides the DFO with the number of people fishing with licenses, without addressing conservation concerns.

However, Justice Millward's findings were not accorded much merit by the BCCA which reversed the findings of the lower courts and found Nikal guilty. The court ruled that such a finding by the lower court was *inconsistent* with *Sparrow,* in which the SCC had decided that the Crown could regulate aboriginal rights. The substance of the BCCA ruling was upheld by the SCC and, almost as an aside, the SCC confirmed that aboriginal peoples had a constitutional right to fish for food and ceremonial purposes. It was at this latter affirmation that aboriginal leaders expressed pleasure. In other words, despite the SCC ruling that substantially went against them, aboriginal leaders found comfort in an issue that was already the case (following the *Sparrow* decision). Herb George, spokesperson for the Wet'suwet'en Hereditary Chiefs, commented that he was pleased with the decision but added, "I see a big policy gap between what the court has said and what the government is doing" (Bell 1996: A1). According to Eric Johnson (1996), fisheries coordinator for the Assembly of First Nations, the Ontario government has rushed to apply the provisions of *Nikal* (i.e., a licensing requirement) but has yet to apply the ruling in *Sparrow*.

There are various possible explanations as to why *Sparrow* has not lived up to the expectations of aboriginal communities. The reasons are complex and multilayered, but two factors are worth noting. First and foremost, fish is a valuable commodity worth billions of dollars; and second, in their fight for fish, aboriginal fishers have come across a formidable opponent—the B.C. Fisheries Council companies and the multinational corporations, which control the commercial fishing industry. In other words, the stakes are very high. These corporations, which directly and indirectly employ thousands of people, have invested hundreds of millions of dollars and have worked hard at developing markets for fish products. Furthermore, the livelihoods of individual commercial fishers and fish plant workers depend on the existence of a viable commercial industry, and they have clearly demonstrated that they will not change to accommodate other user groups, particularly if competing users are allowed to fish first. Compounding this reluctance to change is the federal government policy on unemployment benefits. Those employed in seasonal work, such as fishing, are entitled to collect unemployment benefits during the off season. This system has created a subculture of dependence and, some say, a rather profitable way of life when persons who are employed for part of the year are compensated for the entire year. In 1995, for example, unemployment benefits to fishers totalled $100 million (Howard 1996: D3; Simpson 1996: A24; Marchak 1987).

The financial well-being of the multinationals and their shareholders depends upon a ready and available supply of fish; profitable economic activity requires certainty, predictability, consistency and dependability. It is worth remembering that it was the continued assertion of independence on part of the aboriginal fishers during the early days of the inception of the commercial fishing industry wthat led to company-driven legislation that eventually forced aboriginal peoples into the marginal position in which they find themselves today—the companies forced aboriginal fishers out to control the market. When the power of multinationals is matched against that of an economically and politically marginalized group, it is not difficult to predict the outcome. As documented throughout this study, the odds tend to be stacked against aboriginal peoples, and in the fight for fish the odds have proven insurmountable. It is clear that the multinationals will not concede to the hopes of a powerless and historically disadvantaged minority, no matter what the courts have to say. Aiding and abetting the capitalist interests is the state, which explains the "big gap" of which Herb George spoke. This is evidenced by the DFO's continued violation of the ruling in *Sparrow* for the sake of the profitability of the commercial industry. This in itself is not surprising, since the history of commercial fishing in British Columbia is also the history of government control and marginalization of aboriginal fishers. As documented in Chapter Two and Chapter Four, the state has continually weighed in on behalf of the multinational corporations. At this stage it is worth revisiting the events of August 1995.

Prior to announcing the August 1995 aboriginal-only fishing opening, which raised the ire of the commercial industry, the DFO just a week before had cancelled two scheduled openings for aboriginal fishers. The reason given by the DFO was that there were simply no fish to be caught and conservation of the remaining stocks was paramount. Ernie Crey expressed his disappointment but commented, "We've never been a people to argue against conservation." The Musqueam Indian Band agreed and expressed support for conservation measures. It was clear that the aboriginal community had no choice but to agree for the apparent sake of conservation. The DFO had painted such a bleak picture that any insistence to continue fishing would have been a public relations disaster, and in the fight over fish the battles are also fought in the public arena. The DFO figures for the salmon count seemed so alarmingly low that one industry spokesperson called it a "natural disaster." Brian Tobin, then federal minister responsible for fisheries, flew in from Ottawa to meet industry representatives in Vancouver who in turn told Tobin: "We are appalled that your department is permitting aboriginal commercial fishing to continue . . . despite this conservation crisis."

Typically, the industry intentionally got its facts wrong; the opening was for a food fishery not a commercial one, and the industry is well aware of the difference. However, notwithstanding the apparent conservation crisis, the commercial industry pressured the DFO to allow commercial fishing to continue—the commercial fishers and the multinationals were facing an economic crisis. This left the DFO with an apparent dilemma: how to allow commercial fishing when aboriginal fishing had just been cancelled. And, with the fish counts being so low, how could the DFO allow the commercial fishers to fill their nets? The dilemma was resolved when the DFO suddenly declared that there were more fish than originally thought; in other words, the DFO scientists and bureaucrats were said to have erred in counting the fish. Hence, within a matter of just one week, in a move to appease the commercial users, the DFO revised the original count and now there was no "natural disaster" and enough fish for everyone.

In typical fashion, and in a move reminiscent of the "shadow" effect, the DFO, ostensibly to fulfil its obligations under *Sparrow,* accorded the first opening to aboriginal fishers. However the opening was for only twelve hours and during a time when tides were running out. Even this perceived capitulation by the DFO was too much for the commercial fishers and they amassed in vehement protest. Needless to say, the aboriginal fishers came nowhere close to catching their allocation. However, there were enough fish to allow for conservation and for aboriginal fishers because there was no conservation crisis to begin with. It may have been a "natural disaster" for the commercial fishers, but this should not have prevented the DFO from fulfilling its obligations to the aboriginal fishers. The SCC had emphatically stated that only if there were fish left over after conservation and aboriginal needs had been met, could the other users (i.e., commercial fishers) have access to the resource. But that is not what happened. Following the twelve-hour aboriginal-only fishing, the DFO allowed the commercial fishers, with their immense catching capacity, to fish for twenty-four hours starting the next day (see J. Smith 1995: A5; Crawley 1995b: A1; Cernetig 1995: A4).

The preceding situation clearly called upon the DFO to honour the explicit directives of the SCC. Based on the fish count there should not have been any commercial fishing; there were only sufficient fish to meet the needs of conservation and aboriginal fishers according to the priority order established by the Supreme Court. However, as in previous years, notwithstanding the *Sparrow* decision, the aboriginal fishers were deliberately shortchanged.

The situation today is no different than it was when the *Sparrow* decision was announced and celebrated by aboriginal communities throughout Canada. Aboriginal fishing rights continue to be ignored, and their attempts to exercise those rights continue to be thwarted and frustrated at every turn. Aboriginal fishers are denied access to the resource, and they sit and watch other users who have no constitutional right to the resource take the lion's share. Attempts by aboriginal communities to establish a sustainable economy based on a natural resource that is constitutionally guaranteed to them are met with resistance and roadblocks of an increasingly insidious nature. The DFO has the mandated authority to manage fisheries, but it has no right to subvert the ruling of the Supreme Court of Canada, and that is exactly what it has done.

Recently the British Columbia Court of Appeal had the occasion to examine the principles enunciated in *Sparrow* in three fishing rights cases of *R. v. Sampson and Elliott, R.* v. *Little* and *Regina* v. *Jack, John and John.* The SCC may have narrowly construed section 35(1) of the *Constitution Act, 1982*, but that does not mean that the courts fail to uphold their rulings and legal principles or take kindly to their violation, even though the rulings do allow for flexible interpretation (as was the case when the Supreme Court of British Columbia reviewed the case). In each case, the BCCA applied *Sparrow* and in each case the BCCA concluded that the requirements of *Sparrow* had not been met. For example, the appellants in *Jack, John and John* were all charged with fishing contrary to the *Fisheries Act.* They were caught with five or six live salmon, which were released by the attending fisheries officer; one dead salmon was confiscated and set in motion another expensive court trial initiated by the Crown for the purpose of convicting an aboriginal fisher and protecting the fisheries for commercial users. The Crown, which is legally supposed to act in a trust-like capacity as far as aboriginal relations are concerned, argued for the conviction of the accused.

The trial judge hearing the matter acquitted the accused. In applying the *Sparrow* principles, the judge determined that the DFO had acted arbitrarily in the closure of aboriginal fishing and in the imposition of an allocation for aboriginal fishers. The judge held that the conduct of the DFO did not reflect the supposed trust-like relationship between the government and aboriginal peoples. The judge found that there had been no consultation between the DFO and the aboriginal fishers and that the salmon allocation was divided among the commercial fishers and sport fishers, which resulted in the heaviest burden of conservation being placed upon aboriginal fishers. The judge also found the closure of the river (in effect, a closure of aboriginal fishing) to be a clear violation of Mr. Jack's constitutional rights.

The Crown, again forgetting its trust-like relationship, and supported by the B.C. Fisheries Council and the Pacific Fishermen's Alliance (the intervenors in the case), appealed the decision of the trial judge to the Supreme Court of British Columbia. The Crown argued that the objective of protecting the commercial and sport fisheries from devastation was a valid objective that justified any infringement of the rights enunciated in *Sparrow*. The Supreme Court judge agreed; he also applied the *Sparrow* principles and found Jack, John and John guilty (stating the same reasons for which the accused had been acquitted at trial). The judge found that the closure of the river was valid and stated: "It would not be possible to protect all wild chinook salmon *without serious effects on the commercial fishing industry*" (in *R.* v. *Jack, John and John* 1995: 26, emphasis added).

The judge obviously read into the reasoning of *Sparrow* an issue that had been explicitly removed from consideration, i.e., that the concerns of commercial fisheries are relegated to secondary consideration. However, the judge cannot be entirely faulted. The malleability of legal reasoning allows for varied interpretations and the judge was clearly not blind to the situation of the commercial intervenors in the case as he overturned the decision of the trial judge.

Jack (along with John and John) appealed their convictions to the BCCA. The BCCA agreed with Jack and overturned the guilty verdict. It stated (*R.* v. *Jack, John and John* 1995: 31): "In our opinion, the DFO failed to give priority to Mr. Jack's aboriginal right when it prohibited any fishing for chinook . . . but at the same time allowed sport fishers [to fish for chinook salmon]." In reaching their decision, the BCCA quoted the trial judge with approval:

> [The trial judge] held that such allocations were unilaterally imposed by the DFO and that the Indians were expected to abide by any corresponding regulations and orders. He held that such conduct did

not reflect the trust-like relationship with which the Crown was required to deal with aboriginal peoples. He therefore found that there had not been as little infringement as possible in order to affect the desired conservation result. (in *R. v. Jack, John and John* 1995: 39–40)

The preponderance of facts leads to an inescapable conclusion: the DFO has failed in its constitutional obligations to the aboriginal peoples of Canada. This failure cannot be attributed to an anomalous situation, nor is it an aberration. On the contrary, the failure arises out of a planned and deliberate undermining of *Sparrow,* and it has been carried out in the most sophisticated of manners, leading the aboriginal peoples, the general public and the individual commercial fisher to believe that the DFO is doing its utmost, through, for example, the AFS and PSA, to fulfil its constitutional obligations when in fact it has done the opposite.

The conclusion that the DFO has failed the aboriginal peoples is found not only in this analysis but also in other sources. The B.C. Court of Appeal, in *John, Jack and Jack,* concluded that, in the circumstances of that particular case, the DFO had not lived up to the standard of conduct demanded by *Sparrow.* The David Suzuki Foundation (1995), an environmentalist "think tank," gave the DFO an "F" for "Failure" in its management of aboriginal fisheries; seasoned observers of the fishing industry (for example, Terry Glavin and David Ellis) and even sources within the DFO have reached similar conclusions. A report released by a team of twelve independent consultants hired to review DFO operations concluded that the DFO had misled the public, and it found serious flaws in the way the DFO operates (in Hume 1996a: A1). According to groups involved in the fishing industry, the DFO deliberately underestimates fish stocks in order to mould public opinion (in Bouw 1996: B1). This explains how the DFO is able to move from a situation of a "natural disaster" to a situation where fish counts improve to allow for openings. In another report commissioned by the Steelhead Society of British Columbia, an environmental and sport fishery group, a consultant concluded that commercial fishers are underreporting their catches by up to 30 percent because the DFO has been lax in enforcing its policies (in Crawley 1996a: A4). And, of course, aboriginal peoples themselves, who live with the broken promises of the DFO, are all too familiar with the fact that their rights are not respected. Ernie Crey and Clarence Pennier of the Sto:lo Nation and the numerous Bands who were not permitted to fish for their allocated share in 1992, 1993, 1994 and 1995 can readily attest to the utter failure of the DFO. Aboriginal Bands who are starving because they have not been allowed to fish for food can also attest to the undeniable fact that the ruling in *Sparrow* has been undermined (Pennier 1995; Crey 1998).

In the face of all this, why has the DFO persisted in clinging to the old ways?

## WHY HAS THE DFO FAILED?

Until *Sparrow,* the management of fisheries by the DFO had continued unchanged and on a relatively even keel. Fish in Canada are managed by an army of administrators, scientists and support staff, supposedly secure in the perception that they are managing the resource in accordance with the department's mandate; they are also secure in the knowledge that their unionized jobs have the security of tenure. However, *Sparrow* changed all that. The SCC decision required the DFO to rethink the way it did business and to drastically change the way fisheries are managed.

The DFO had been accustomed to bullying aboriginal fishers and telling them when, where and how to fish, and how much to catch. Most of all, the DFO had become quite cozy with the B.C. Fisheries Council companies and had developed its own culture and a monolithic bureaucratic organization to match. In 1981–82 the total budget of the Pacific Region of the DFO was $84 million (Pearse 1982: 234); in 1993–94 the budget was $147.8 million (Schwindt 1996: 113); in 1994–95 it was $241 million (O'Neil 1996b). A significant percentage of the budget is allocated to salaries for an army of bureaucrats who have a vested interest in continuing the status quo (Marchak 1987: 17). In 1996 there were 2,300 employees in the Pacific Region and 1,327 employees in the head office for a total of 10,367 in all of Canada (O'Neil 1996). Based on DFOs 1981–82 budget, Marchak (1987: 17) concluded that the cost of managing fisheries is close or equivalent to the commercial value of the fish. Applying more recent figures, Schwindt (1996: 114) concluded that the combined government expenditure in managing the fisheries and investment by the private sector has greatly exceeded the commercial value of the fish. In other words, the fisheries cost more than they generate in monetary return. Carl Walters, a fisheries biologist at the University of British Columbia, is even more critical (in Alden 1996: A19): "The fishery has become a pathetic drain on public resources, almost certainly costing the public more than it returns in terms of employment and social benefits."

If the DFO were a private enterprise, one would expect some serious restructuring of its organization, such as loss of jobs, in line with the financial realities. However, the unionized positions of DFO employees makes it difficult to eliminate jobs and hence the organization continues on its present course.

The DFO has resisted meeting the directives of the SCC or adapting to the evolving environment in which it operates. According to Chief Joe Becker (1996) and an anonymous senior DFO manager, there is resistance at every level, from fisheries officers to senior managers. Mr. Becker notes that there has been some genuine cooperation at the higher levels, but the same cannot be said of the staff at lower levels, and he ascribes this to a concern over jobs. A senior manager at the DFO ascribes the resistance to change to a concern about jobs as well as systemic racism within the DFO, i.e., persons who have managed with a particular perception maintain that perception even when it is not supported by facts. It is worth noting that aboriginal fishers have long considered the DFO as public enemy number one (Newell 1993). DFO bureaucrats also face conflicting directives; the courts tell them to do one thing, but their managers tell them to do something else. How else can one explain the continued violation of the *Sparrow* decision?

Whatever the reason for the DFO's resistance to change or reluctance to accept the ruling of the SCC, it is apparent that *Sparrow* has created a siege mentality among DFO staff. The B.C. Fisheries Survival Coalition receives and has received hundreds of tips in the form of confidential "leaked" information regarding aboriginal fisheries. Disgruntled DFO employees motivated possibly by racism or a concern over possible job loss have provided the Survival Coalition with considerable ammunition with which to battle aboriginal fisheries; a representative of the coalition showed me a stack of confidential internal information leaked to him by DFO staff. Perhaps this resistance also explains the AFS program, which was ostensibly designed to address the *Sparrow* decision but has in fact addressed the need of the DFO, and the needs of the DFO have always been concerned with the profitability of the commercial industry. As one anonymous DFO employee stated, the AFS buys back the authority supposedly lost because of *Sparrow* and allows the DFO to continue operating as it has in the past.

Not only is there concern over job loss within the DFO, there is also concern over job loss within the commercial fishing industry. Indirectly and directly, the fishing industry in B.C. employs thousands of people and many coastal communities depend on fish for their survival. Millions of dollars of investment by both the public and private sector are tied up in fishing. Ironically this capitalization, or overcapitalization, is the cause of many of the ills pervading the commercial industry. When politicians are pressed with such issues involving profound economic and social implications, they listen, and the rights of a marginalized people pale in comparison—no matter that the concerns of aboriginal peoples are equally, if not more, pressing.

As noted earlier, the DFO is not entirely to blame. The department is under constant and intense pressure to submit to the needs of the commercial fishery. The DFO is under constant scrutiny by commercial fishers, who have demonstrated an unwillingness to tolerate any incursions into what they view as their territory. Complicating matters is the fact that fishing is heavily subsidized by unemployment benefits and by taxpayer-funded grants to various groups that lobby on behalf of the commercial industry, indicating the paradoxical nature of the milieu in which the DFO operates. Many of these grants are awarded to B.C. Fisheries Council companies, including B.C. Packers and the Canadian Fishing Company. These grants are not repayable and amount to hundreds of thousands of dollars. For 1991 and 1992, they totalled almost one million dollars (in Glavin 1996c: 15).

Commercial fishers in New Brunswick have gathered outside the home of the provincial fisheries minister and pelted his home with eggs and other projectiles. Fishers have occupied DFO offices, wrapped DFO offices in fishing nets, closed the street around DFO offices by stringing nets across the street, vandalized the property of aboriginal fishers, swamped aboriginal boats and organized what amounts to a virtual hate campaign against aboriginal fishing. They have also initiated countless lawsuits against the DFO and its senior managers. Fishers have become the proverbial thorn in the side of the DFO.

In addition to these pressures, the DFO must also be responsive to systemic requirements. In essence, the DFO must help to fulfil the state's function of aiding in the accumulation process. According to Marchak (1987: 18–19), it is in the service of this function that the state takes an active role in containing conflict between various user groups. The continuing and intense conflict between aboriginal and commercial fishers necessitates state intervention. The state cannot afford interruptions to a vital economic activity; it is the state's function to maintain profitable conditions in any given industry. And faced with the immense power wielded by the multinational corporations, the state invariably resolves the conflict in favour of the powerful because it can ill afford to do otherwise (Marchak 1987: 11).

## IS RIGHTS LITIGATION AN EFFECTIVE TOOL?
In deciding *Sparrow,* the SCC did not offer a remedy or even begin to redress historical wrongs; the judges merely suggested a method for sharing the resource. It appears that the court relied on rhetorical appeasement to set the tone and, in doing so, misled the litigants. The victory celebrated by aboriginal communities is illustrative of a perception of having won, when the SCC actually set out a framework on how to control section 35(1) rights. In doing so, the SCC dealt a severe blow to the aspirations of aboriginal peoples by limiting the scope of the rights envisioned by section 35(1). It should be recalled that the aboriginal peoples initially lobbied against the constitutional exercise preceding the repatriation of 1982, fearing that they had nothing to gain and much to lose. This view was of course based on previous dealings with the government where aboriginal peoples have consistently come up short. After much soul-searching, the aboriginal leaders decided to participate in the process and lobbied equally hard to ensure that the protection envisioned by section 35(1) was placed beyond the reach of the limitations (as per section 1) and the notwithstanding clause (section 33) of the *Charter.* However, the SCC imported into its analysis an interpretative guideline that provides other courts the means with which to limit section 35(1) protection. As Berger (1989: 606) noted, the limiting analysis was invented out of thin air.

This case study of *Sparrow* is not offered as proof for either side of the debate concerning the transformative capacity of law. Based on my own findings, I cannot offer anything more than a qualified and cautious support for the strategy of litigating rights. Arguably it does lead to change, as an analogy can illustrate. Picture a giant block of wood representing the status quo. Poised to strike this block is a chisel being held by a subordinate group, and this chisel can be propelled forward only by positive court rulings. Each positive decision propels the chisel forward and, for the motion to continue, successive positive court decisions must follow. In other words, rights litigation is like slowly chipping away at the status quo in order to gain entry into mainstream society. This analogy, or the premise, was personally suggested to me in 1995 by Louise Mandell, author, lawyer and strong advocate of aboriginal rights. It is Ms. Mandell who took the *Vanderpeet* case to the SCC *(Vanderpeet* attempts to further the aims of *Sparrow* and deals with the commercial use of aboriginal "rights" fishery).

The proper question then becomes not whether the law is capable of transforming existing relations of subordination and domination, but whether it is an *effective* strategy for doing so in this case.

There are two concerns with the above analogy. First, there is always the possibility that the court will decide against you (as happened in the major fishing rights cases of *Vanderpeet, Gladstone, N.T.C. Smokehouse, Nikal* and, contrary to popular belief, *Sparrow).* In other words, the strategy can backfire. Second, and perhaps more important, how effective a strategy is it? Court challenges take years to resolve, and can cost millions of dollars. For subordinate groups, resources are scarce to begin with and they cannot afford to direct valuable resources towards a strategy that has produced and continues to produce negligible results. Consider once again the case of *Sparrow*: the court challenge was initiated in 1984, was not decided until six years later, and did not produce anything that substantially improves the access to fish. The one issue that has become a focal point involves the sale of fish under the provisions of the *Pilot Sales Agreement.* However, *Sparrow* has nothing to do with the PSA.

The real story is found in the boardrooms of the DFO and at the strategy meetings in various aboriginal communities. According to one observer, members of the Nuu-chah-nulth Tribe challenged the DFO for restricting their ability to sell fish caught under food fish provisions; a spokesperson for the Nuu-chah-nulth made it clear to a senior DFO manager that they would continue to sell and the only way to stop the practice was to arrest each and every Nuu-chah-nulth.[8] Faced with the daunting prospect of massive civil disobedience, having to arrest hundreds of aboriginal fishers and the potential political fallout, the DFO backed down. Even so, the DFO still emerged victorious because the PSA was only signed with four out of more than ninety aboriginal Bands in B.C. and, more importantly, did not increase the amount of fish that could be caught (Ellis 1996). In any event, the last laugh in this matter must be accorded to the commercial industry. Recently the DFO announced that it will suspend the PSA and allow a continuance of the PSA only on the condition that there be a commercial fishery in waters where aboriginal fishing takes place (reported by Crawley 1996b: B1).

Reliance on litigation distracts from other, potentially more effective tactics. In addition to the fact that lengthy court challenges are costly and time-consuming, litigating for rights can also provide an excuse for politicians *not* to act to resolve issues that are essentially political questions, not legal. Politicians can demur from taking action while seeking refuge by awaiting a court's decision. Meanwhile the suffering and inequity will continue.

In liberal-democratic societies, however, one cannot overlook the importance of law. Winning legal battles legitimizes one's attempts to challenge the status quo. It accords to one's struggle the undeniable cachet that ones' actions are condoned by law, and if not condoned, then at least supported as far as legality is concerned. Has legitimizing the struggle by aboriginal peoples accorded any benefits? Not apparently so, judging by what is happening in the fishing waters. White commercial fishers disrupt aboriginal peoples in the peaceful exercise of their constitutional rights, and no one is arrested or charged. Even more alarming is the undeniable fact that the DFO has continually violated the ruling in *Sparrow.* Even this small victory has been undermined. The DFO has consistently and blatantly ignored the principles of the decision and the explicit directives of the court. The DFO has taken the narrowest possible interpretation of the decision and has turned the tables in its own favour. There is a lesson in this: if the state considers it acceptable to violate aboriginal constitutional rights, then why should other users not consider it acceptable to violate aboriginal rights also? As demonstrated by the actions of individual commercial fishers and the multinationals, that is exactly what is happening in the fishing waters throughout Canada.

It is worth repeating that aboriginal peoples are legally entitled to first priority only when fishing for food, social and ceremonial purposes. This ruling provides considerable flexibility for the state to further limit access to the resource. The ultimate prize in the battle was a right to harvest fish commercially, but this was denied by the SCC because it refused to deal with the issue, even though it was clear to the most casual of observers that this issue is what the case was about.

In this current era of rights discourse (Mandel 1989, 1996) everyone seems concerned about special status or rights and whether one group or person is accorded more rights than others, no matter how abstract or intangible those rights may be; and the issue makes for heated debates. Somehow, accordance of rights to aboriginal peoples—rights that are constitutionally guaranteed and recognize past injustices—are being construed or purposefully misconstrued as the granting of special privileges to the detriment of others. Opponents focus on them as an affront and react with outrage. Politicians pick up the phrase "special status," the news media repeats it and the issue takes on a life of its own; newspaper columnists and radio talk-show hosts speak of "apartheid"; and lobbyists speak of "racial segregation" and complain that aboriginal peoples are getting all the rights. There is not one iota of evidence to suggest that aboriginal peoples are being given special rights. There is considerable evidence to the contrary, but the issue of special status or rights keeps cropping up. *British Columbia Reports* (1996), a right-wing newsmagazine boldly declared on its front cover that democracy has been denied in British Columbia because the provincial government has not agreed to the demands of certain protestors to call a referendum on the Nisga'a agreement. (The commercial users are outraged that the agreement contains provisions for a Nisga'a-managed fishery on the Nass River, which runs through the reserve.)

## CONCLUSION

The aboriginal peoples of Canada remain on the outside looking in, and it appears that that is where they will remain for some time to come.

When the leaders of the top economic nations, or the Group of Seven (G7), met in Halifax to discuss economic issues in the summer of 1995, Ovide Mercredi, First Chief of the Assembly of First Nations (AFN), led a group of protestors in a symbolic attempt to crash the summit and publicize the plight of aboriginal peoples. Mr. Mercredi and the other protestors were turned away by a cordon of security officers, but not before Mercredi condemned the Canadian government for denying aboriginal rights to hunt and fish before the international media representatives gathered to cover the summit.

About a year later, Mercredi was again denied the opportunity to participate in another crucial conference involving all the provincial governments and the federal government. The chief of the AFN wrote to the prime minister (in correspondence dated April 24, 1996) urging that aboriginal leaders be allowed to participate to discuss issues of profound importance to aboriginal peoples, but to no avail.

In 1996, the entire staff of commissioners of the federal Indian Specific Claims Commission resigned to protest government inaction. The commissioners stated that they did not wish to further frustrate aboriginal aspirations by holding out hopes of settlements, and they said their work was being "severely undermined" by a lack of government response (Canadian Press 1996a).

Meanwhile, the Mi'kmaq of Nova Scotia have decided that enough is enough and established a commission to oversee hunting and fishing in Mi'kmaq territory. A spokesperson stated: "We have decided to . . . regulate our own rights . . . we are getting tired of people going to court fighting over rights and access to certain resources" (Canadian Press, May 21, 1996).

The 1995 fishing season was a watershed of things to come. It was clearly one of the worst fishing seasons on record with all users suffering losses. However, the group that is legally not supposed to bear the brunt suffered the most. Aboriginal leader Ernie Crey's comments on the 1995 season is to the point: "This hit to our economy could only be described as staggering . . . the larders of our families will be very nearly empty" (in Cernetig 1996: A4).

And the larders of many aboriginal families, particularly those in remote and isolated reserves, were empty. All indications were that the larders will also be empty in 1996. The DFO again manipulated the allocation quota of salmon for aboriginal Bands, again without consulting the Bands as required by the *Sparrow* decision. According to Ken Malloway of the Sto:lo Nation, the DFO waited until the last possible minute to inform the aboriginal Bands of the change in allocation: "They . . . deliberately delayed letting us know so that we wouldn't have time to challenge them" (in Smith 1996: 7). The delay in informing the aboriginal Bands about changes in allocation allowed the commercial fishers to catch fish that should have been either caught by the aboriginal fishers or allowed to escape for spawning.

By all indications, the situation will worsen in the years to come. The DFO initiated two controversial programs for the fishing industry and both these programs do not serve the interests or needs of aboriginal fishing communities. The catch-and-release program for sport fishers allows sport fishing to continue while aboriginal fishers are prohibited from fishing. The Haida, citing a 30–50 percent mortality rate of the catch-and-release fish, recently lost a legal bid to stop the fishing. They sought an injunction on the grounds that it was unconstitutional for the DFO to allow sport fishing while prohibiting them from fishing for food.

Of the two programs, the most controversial is the so-called "Mifflin Plan," named after a former federal minister in charge of fisheries. The plan has been severely criticized by individual commercial fishers and their respective unions for catering to the needs of the B.C. Fisheries Council companies and increasing the "corporatization" of fishing (Howard 1996: D3). According to Glavin (1996c: 13), the Mifflin Plan has accorded to B.C.'s biggest fishing companies everything they requested. A report commissioned by the B.C. government concludes that the Mifflin Plan will have a devastating effect on fishing communities and states (in McLintock 1996: A2): "Many of these are aboriginal communities with few alternative employment prospects." In spite of these objections the Mifflin Plan was to go into effect, even though experts in the field noted that the plan does nothing for conservation and everything to cater to the interests of the powerful corporations. To this criticism, the person responsible for the implementation of the Mifflin Plan responds, "I can't see any real downside to letting market efficiencies prevail" (in Howard 1996: D3).

In Ontario, which has not applied the principles of *Sparrow,* the bullying of aboriginal fishers continues. Michael Valpy of the *Globe and Mail* ponders: "I want to understand something. Why year after year, do the Chippewas of Nawash have to fight off their provincial government, thieves, arsonists . . . including local (politicians) to catch fish?" (1996: A17). In August 1995 a mob of about seventy fishers harassed a Chippewa woman selling fish and threw fish entrails at her; a Nawash fish boat that had been sunk and later raised was set ablaze while it was docked at a federal dock; during the same time, 10,000 metres of commercial nets belonging to the Chippewa were stolen and vandalized. When asked to respond, a member of the Ontario legislature surmised that it could be the Chippewa themselves who had vandalized and burned their own property "or somebody from Russia" (in Valpy 1996: A17).

This is indeed a sad and deplorable state of affairs with no resolution in sight. What the aboriginal fishers want is not "special treatment," "special status," "special rights" or any other pejoratively imbued terms ascribed to their quest for a recognition of their rights. Aboriginal peoples have sought from the courts a restoration of rights once enjoyed by them without obstruction or hindrance. The aboriginal demands expressed during my conversations with Chief Joe Becker (1995 and 1996) and others involved in aboriginal issues do not seem unreasonable and are not exclusionary. What aboriginals have sought is a level playing field, not favouritism; what they seek is respect for their constitutional rights. However, what is going on in the fishing waters of B.C. has nothing to do with respect for aboriginal traditions, history or rights. It also has nothing to do with conservation, in spite of overwhelming evidence of a rapid decline in salmon stocks. Furthermore, it has nothing to do with fairness or justice, and it most certainly has nothing to do with *Sparrow*. It does have everything to do with racism, greed and political expediency: racism in the form of a united front against aboriginal fishers, the propagation of false and inflammatory information, a deliberate ignorance of the *Sparrow* decision and a deliberate denial of historical and legal rights; greed in the form of fishing for profit and the plundering of the resource, and a concerted effort to keep others (particularly aboriginal fishers) out of the lucrative commercial market; and political expediency in the form of the DFO's continued capitulation to moneyed interests.

When I first embarked on this research, I expected to reach a different conclusion. At first glance, all indications pointed to a very positive interpretation and application of the principles enunciated in *Sparrow*. There were indications that the government was doing all it could, in an expeditious manner, to respond to the Supreme Court of Canada decision. Furthermore, an initial reading of the SCC decision, with its grandiloquent statements about mistreatment of aboriginal peoples, seemed almost enlightened—for the first time, the highest court in the land was admitting that the First Peoples of Canada have not been treated fairly. Based on this, I prematurely concluded that the law can indeed assist the disadvantaged to achieve a measure of social justice or equality, that the law can even the odds. However, upon further research and critical analysis, my initial opinion gave way to disappointment and outrage.

There is something profoundly wrong and unjust happening in the fishing waters of B.C. and Canada. The only fair and proper response would be to allow unhindered and free access to the resource. Aboriginal fishers should have the unequivocal freedom of choice to do with the fish whatever best suits their needs: sell them or use them for food or social and ceremonial purposes.

However, I am also wearily pragmatic and cynical and I do not foresee any favourable resolution for the aboriginal fisher. It appears that not only the federal government but also the general public have hardened in their attitudes towards aboriginal peoples. A recent survey commissioned by the federal government concludes that attitudes towards aboriginal issues have changed significantly, particularly when compared to a similar survey conducted only two years ago. According to the more recent survey, a majority of Canadians feel that aboriginal peoples are being unreasonable in their demands to settle land claims; the figure for B.C. is 67 percent. More than 40 percent of Canadians feel that aboriginal peoples have themselves to blame for their problems (in Aubury 1996: A4). In view of this, it is difficult to be optimistic.

In any event, it is not improbable that the fight over fish may amount to naught for there is a growing likelihood that commercially valuable fish, which have lived in B.C. waters for countless years, may soon be extinct; that is, unless drastic measures are taken to conserve the remaining stocks. But the manner in which the DFO has managed the fish, and the incurable greed exhibited by those in the commercial industry, does not provide much reason to hope for a miracle, which is what is needed for the fish to survive.

## POSTSCRIPT

On August 22, 1996, following the completion of this study, the Supreme Court of Canada decided three cases dealing with aboriginal fishing rights: *R. v. Vanderpeet, R. v. N.T.C. Smokehouse* and *R. v. Gladstone.*[9] In the first two cases, the SCC ruled against the aboriginal appellants, and in *Gladstone* the SCC ruled in favour of the Heiltsuk peoples and ordered a new trial.

Almost immediately following the announcements by the SCC, members of the B.C. Fisheries Survival Coalition started celebrating. In keeping with their disruptive tactics, the coalition members convened in an area where an opening for aboriginal-only fishing was taking place, and began to fish. "This is only the beginning," stated Phil Eidsvik, director of the Survival Coalition. He called for an immediate halt of the Aboriginal Fisheries Strategy and demanded that the fisheries component of the Nisga'a agreement be rescinded.

There is no doubt that the SCC has dealt a severe, if not a knockout, blow to aboriginal aspirations. In the most important of the three cases, *Vanderpeet,* the SCC ruled against the Sto:lo Nation, stating that the Band had not proven that the practice of bartering fish was a central or integral part of Sto:lo society. The court stated:

> The facts do not support the appellant's claim . . . the findings of fact . . . suggest that the exchange of salmon for money or goods, while certainly taking place in Sto:lo society prior to contact, was not a sig-nificant, integral or defining feature of that society . . . the appellant has failed to demonstrate that (the barter in salmon) is an aboriginal right . . . under s. 35(1) of the *Constitution Act, 1982.* (*R. v. Vanderpeet* 1996)

The irony of the court coming to this decision should be obvious: a group of nine men and women, all white, all conservative and all over the age of fifty-five deciding what is central to an aboriginal society. The same court in *Sparrow* had ruled that the aboriginal perspective must be taken into account when determining what is an aboriginal right. In view of the preceding decisions, it is difficult to state with any confidence that Supreme Court justices are capable of appreciating such a perspective.

In deciding *Vanderpeet,* the SCC did leave open the possibility that aboriginal fishers may have the right to sell their fish, providing they can prove that right in law. However, that is the crux of the problem. If the Sto:lo and the Nuu-chah-nulth (*N.T.C. Smokehouse),* for whom salmon is central, cannot prove that they possess that right, how can other Bands do so? In my view, the SCC has set up an almost insurmountable test and has, in effect, offered a false hope. The decision encourages litigation because Bands that have fished from time immemorial do not doubt that they possess the right to do what they wish with the fish, including selling them. The Sto:lo and the Nuu-chah-nulth spent an enormous amount of money—according to Chief Steven Point (1996), the Sto:lo Nation spent over $250,000 in the *Vanderpeet* case—waited eight long years for an answer and lost.

Even more troubling, from an aboriginal perspective, was the SCC decision in *Gladstone.* William and Donald Gladstone were convicted of selling herring spawn without a proper license. The SCC ruled that the Gladstone brothers were exercising an aboriginal right when they sold the herring spawn on kelp, but it did not rule whether the licensing scheme infringed that right and ordered a new trial. However, the court also stated:

> Where the aboriginal right has no internal limitation . . . some limitation of those rights will be justifiable . . . [in the interests of] regional and economic fairness, and the recognition of the historical reliance upon, and participation in, the fishery by non-aboriginal groups. (*R.* v. *Gladstone* 1996)

It is clear that the *Gladstone* decision provides a means for the state to further restrict aboriginal rights and distribute the fish as it sees fit in the interests of "regional and economic fairness." As documented in the preceding pages, that criteria translates into what is best for white fishers and multinational corporations.

Once again the SCC rulings are being hailed as "landmark" by the news media, lawyers and academics. However, the question remains: "landmark" for whom?

It is also important to keep these decisions in perspective. Even if the aboriginal appellants (in *Vanderpeet* and *N.T.C. Smokehouse)* had won, it would not have changed a central fact: the DFO controls the allocation and management of fish. And it is worth remembering that the aboriginal share of the sockeye salmon is a mere 3 percent. It is cold comfort to have the right to sell fish when there is a sharp limitation on how much fish can be caught in the first place.

In sum, these new decisions are likely to bring the same old results.

# Notes

1.  This analysis is limited to aboriginal bands located in the Lower Fraser River region and on Vancouver Island who were signatories to the Aboriginal Fisheries Strategy (AFS). Information from the Department of Fisheries and Oceans on other bands was not made available to me.
2.  The commercial fishing industry does not constitute a homogenous group. In this book, the commercial sector is so identified in order to differentiate it from the aboriginal "rights" fishery. The commercial industry consists of various players (multinational corporations, individual fishers, aboriginal commercial fishers, plant workers); the relationships are complex and characterized by cooperation, acrimony, conflict and competition among and between the various users of the resource. Sport fishers are part of the commercial industry.
3.  It should be noted that the relationship among and between various user groups is complex. While acrimony and conflict has been the rule, there are exceptions driven by grass-roots community campaigns, such as the West Coast Sustainability Association and the Coastal Communities Network (Glavin 1996c: 13), where genuine cooperation and harmonious working relationship exists between aboriginal fishers, sport fishers, white commercial fishers and the multinational corporations (Menzies 1996).
4.  *Constitution Act, 1867*, sections 91(12) and (24).
5.  This information was provided by DFO officials on condition of anonymity.
6.  This was confidential information provided on the assurance of anonymity.
7.  This was the case under the GATT (General Agreement on Tariffs and Trade); it was also ratified in the Free Trade Agreement.
8.  It should be noted that Bruce Rawson, the most senior non-elected DFO official, denies the above incident. Mr. Rawson, now a private consultant in Ottawa, does acknowledge receiving threats but states that the DFO receives hundreds of threats from all parties involved in fishing. Rawson stated that the DFO responded to *Sparrow* in keeping with its constitutional obligations. When I pointed out that my research had concluded that was not the case, Rawson disagreed with my conclusions and stated that the government cannot shirk constitutional obligations (personal communication, June 1996).
9.  These decisions had not yet been reported and were retrieved from the Supreme Court of Canada website.

# Appendix

## Cases Cited

*R.* v. *Adolph* (1983), 47 B.C.L.R. 330 (B.C.C.A.)

*R.* v. *Agawa* [1988], 3 C.N.L.R. 73

*R.* v. *Andrews* (1990), 61 C.C.C. (3d) 490

*Calder* v. *A.-G. of B.C.* [1973], S.C.R. 313

*Delgamuuk* v. *British Columbia,*(B.C.S.C.) 1991, 3 W.W.R. 97; (B.C.C.A.) 1993, 5 W.W.R. 97

*R.* v. *Derriksan* (1976), 31 C.C.C. (2d) 575

*R.* v. *Gladstone* (1993), 80 B.C.L.R. (2d) 133

*R.* v. *Gladstone* [1996], 2 S.C.R. 723

*Guerin* v. *The Queen* (1985), 1 C.N.L.R. 120

*Jack* v. *The Queen* [1980], 1 S.C.R. 294

*R.* v. *Jack, John and John* (now reported), decision dated December 20, 1995

*Johnson* v. *M'Intosh* 8 Wheaton 543 (1823)

*R.* v. *Lewis* 1996 (now reported), S.C.C. File No. 23802

*R.* v. *Little* (now reported), decision dated December 20, 1995

*R.* v. *Morgentaler* [1988], 1 S.C.R. 30

*R.* v. *Nikal* (1996) (now reported), S.C.C. File No. 23804

*R.* v. *N.T.C. Smokehouse Ltd.* (1993), 80 B.C.L.R. (2d) 158

*R.* v. *N.T.C. Smokehouse Ltd.* [1996], 2 S.C.R. 672

*Nowegijick* v. *The Queen* (1983), 144 D.L.R. (3d) 193

*R.* v. *Oakes* (1986), 50 C.R. (3d) 1 (S.C.C.)

*St. Catherines Milling and Lumber Co.* v. *The Queen* (1888), 14 A.C. 46 (P.C.)

*R.* v. *Sampson and Elliott* (now reported) decision dated December 20, 1995

*R.* v. *Simon* [1985], 2 S.C.R. 387

*R.* v. *Sioui* [1990], 1 S.C.R. 1025

*Sparrow* v. *R. et al.* [1987], 2 W.W.R. 577 (B.C.C.A.)

*R.* v. *Sparrow* [1990], 1 S.C.R. 1075

*R.* v. *Vanderpeet* (1993), 80 B.C.L.R. (2d) 75

*R.* v. *Vanderpeet* [1996], 2 S.C.R. 507

# References

Alden, E. 1996. "To save our salmon." *Vancouver Sun,* July 26, A19.

Anderson, C. 1996. "Greenpeace goes fishing." *Vancouver Province,* June 14, A2.

Asch, M., and P. MacKlem. 1991. "Aboriginal Rights and Canadian Sovereignty: An Essay on R. v. Sparrow." *Alberta Law Review* 29:2, 498–517.

Aubury, J. 1996. "Society less tolerant of aboriginal than two years ago, poll indicates." *Vancouver Sun,* July 8, A4.

Barkin, I. 1990. "Aboriginal Rights: A Shell Without the Filling." *Queen's Law Journal* 15, 307–25.

Barnett, C. 1993. "The Tortuous Journey." Unpublished paper.

_____. 1995. "Tales from the Turkey Farm." Unpublished paper.

Barron, S. 1990. "Justice: Where two cultures are divided." *Vancouver Sun,* October 17, B1.

Bartlett, R. 1990. "Resource Development and the Extinguishment of Aboriginal Title in Canada and Australia." *Western Australia Law Review* 20, 453–88.

Beatty, D. 1990. "Supreme Court redone in conservative hues." *Globe and Mail,* April 19, A7.

Becker, J. 1996, 1995. Interview notes, Chief, Musqueam Indian Band, Vancouver, B.C.

Bell, S. 1996. "Fishing group urges NDP defeat over land claims." *Vancouver Sun,* May 7, B1.

_____. 1996. "Indian bands don't control rivers, court rules." *Vancouver Sun,* April 26, A1.

Berger, T.R. 1991. *A Long and Terrible Shadow.* Vancouver: Douglas and MacIntyre.

_____. 1989. "The Charter: A Historical Perspective." *University of British Columbia Law Review,* 23:3,603).

_____. 1981. *Fragile Freedoms.* Vancouver: Clarke Irwin & Company.

Bindman, S. 1996. "Trust in courts grow with wealth." *Vancouver Sun,* July 18, B1.

Binnie, W.I.C. 1990. "The Sparrow Doctrine." *Queen's Law Journal* 15:1–2, 217–45.

Bouw, B. 1996. "Shown low on purpose." *Vancouver Sun,* August 7, B1.

Brannigan, A. 1984. *Crimes, Courts and Corrections.* Toronto: Holt, Rinehart and Winston.

Brickey, S., and E. Comack. 1989. "The Role of Law in Social Transformation." In Caputo et al. (eds.), *Law, State and Society.* Toronto: Harcourt Brace Jovanvich.

_____. 1986. *The Social Basis of Law.* Toronto: Garamond.

British Columbia. 1993. *The 1993 British Columbia Seafood Industry Year in Review.* Ministry of Agriculture, Fisheries and Food.

_____. 1991. *Fisheries Production Statistics of British Columbia.* Ministry of Agriculture, Fisheries and Food.

_____. undated, c. 1990–91. *Commercial Fisheries in B.C.* Ministry of Agriculture, Fisheries and Food.

British Columbia Fisheries Survival Coalition. 1994. "The Aboriginal Fisheries Strategy and the B.C. Fishing Industries." Pamphlet, May 12.

British Columbia Reports. 1996. "Democracy Denied." Cover story, April 16.
Bryden, J. 1991. "Siddon denies he could have prevented stand-off." *Ottawa Sun,* May 3, A3.
Canadian Broadcasting Corporation (CBC). 1995. CBC-CBUFT regional newscast, August 16. Vancouver, B.C.
Canadian Humans Rights Commission. 1994. Annual report. Ottawa: Ministry of Supply and Services.
Canadian Press. 1996a. "Fed-up land claims commissioners quit en masse." *Vancouver Sun,* July 15, A5.
_____ . 1996b. "Haida to appeal fishing law." *Globe and Mail,* July 2, A4.
_____ . 1992a. "Quebec Cree takes fight into courts." *Globe and Mail,* March 30, A5.
_____ . 1992b. "Canada in Top 3 when it comes to jailing people." *Globe and Mail,* February 20, A3
_____ . 1991. "Mohawk loses bid for trial in English." *Globe and Mail,* April 16, A1.
Caputo, T.C., et al. 1989. *Law and Society: A Critical Perspective.* Toronto: Harcourt Brace Jovanovich.
Carter, Sarah. 1990. *Lost Harvests: Prairie Indian Reserve Farmers and Government Policy.* Montreal: McGill-Queen's University Press.
Cassidy, F. 1990. "Introduction." Papers from "The Sparrow Case" conference, November 19. Victoria, B.C.
Cernetig, M. 1996. "Racial tempers rise in salmon dispute." *Globe and Mail,* August 17, A4.
_____ . 1995. "Sport Fishing in B.C." *Report on Business Magazine, Globe and Mail,* September.
Chemainus Tribal Council. 1995. Correspondence to Brian Tobin, Minister of Fisheries and Oceans, August 23.
_____ . 1994. Correspondence to Jean Chretien, Prime Minister of Canada, August 10.
Copes, P. 1995. "The Profits of Justice." Unpublished paper.
Cotterrell, R. 1984. *The Sociology of Law.* London, U.K.: Butterworths.
Crawley, M. 1996a. "Commercial fishers underreporting accidental catches." *Vancouver Sun,* July 17, A4.
_____ . 1996b. "Indians to face ban on sales of salmon." *Vancouver Sun,* June 14, B1.
_____ . 1995a. "Violence threatened as Indians resume fishing." *Vancouver Sun,* August 17, A1.
_____ . 1995b. "Fishing disaster sparks closure." *Vancouver Sun,* August 10, A1.
_____ . 1995c. "Indian fishery opening criticized." *Vancouver Sun,* August 9, B2.
Crey, E. 1998. Personal communication. Director of Fisheries for Sto:lo Nation.
Dafoe, J. 1992. "Sorry, Quebec, sympathy vote must go to aboriginal." *Globe and Mail,* June 20, D2.
_____ . 1991. "Manitoba's Inquiry into Aboriginal Justice merits vastly more than wariness." *Globe and Mail,* September 7, D2.
_____ . 1991. "Canadians are finally hearing the native drums." *Globe and Mail,* June 15, D2.
David Suzuki Foundation. 1995. "Annual Report on Fishing in B.C." Vancouver.
Delacourt, S. 1991. "Ottawa assailed for native program cuts." *Globe and Mail,* January 22, A4.
Department of Fisheries and Oceans (DFO). 1995. *AFS Deskbook.* Pacific Region, Vancouver, B.C., January.

# References

_____. 1993. *West Coast Fisheries: Changing Times.* Catalogue no. Fs 23-240/1993E. Ottawa: Supply and Services Canada.

_____. 1990. Internal memorandum, July 25.

_____. 1989. *Indian Fishing Rights in Canada.* Vancouver.

Doyle-Bedwell, P. 1993. "The Evolution of the Legal Test of Extinguishment from Sparrow to Gitskan." *Canadian Journal of Women and the Law* 6, 193–204.

Duncan, W. 1996, 1995. Interview notes. Senior Administrative Officer, Department of Fisheries and Oceans, Vancouver, B.C.

Eidsvik, P. 1995. Interview notes. Director, B.C. Fisheries Survival Coalition, Vancouver, B.C.

Elliott, D.W. 1991. "In the Wake of Sparrows: A New Department of Fisheries." *University of New Brunswick Law Journal* 40, 23–43.

Ellis, D. 1995 and 1996. Interview notes.

Emerson, T.I. 1989. "Law as a Form for Social Progress." *Connecticut Law Review* 18:1, 1–5.

Fagan, D. 1987a. "Indians tell of injustices in Nova Scotia Courts." *Globe and Mail,* November 3, A1.

_____. 1987b. "Racism alive, all too well, Nova Scotia Indians say." *Globe and Mail,* November 2, A1.

*Financial Post.* 1990. "Oka spectacle endangers Quebec nationalism." November 7.

Fine, S. 1995. "Equal-Rights law victories ring hollow for some groups." *Globe and Mail,* April 17, A1.

_____. 1993. "Scales of justice tilt towards power." *Globe and Mail,* November 6, A1.

_____. 1992. "The Rights Revolution." *Globe and Mail,* November 25, A1.

Foster, C. 1992. "Where the colour of money is white." *Globe and Mail,* November 5, A23.

Fraser, G., and G. Allen. 1991. "Natives seek Equality with Quebec." *Globe and Mail,* August 20, A5.

Freedman, R. 1994. "Aboriginal and Treaty Rights." Course material for Law 353, Fall 1994. Faculty of Law, University of British Columbia, Vancouver: B.C.

Frideres, J.S. 1988. *Native Peoples in Canada: Contemporary Conflicts.* 3rd ed. Scarborough: Prentice-Hall.

Fudge, J. 1992. "Evaluating Rights Litigation as a Form of Transformative Feminist Politics." *Canadian Journal of Law and Society* 7:1, 153–61.

_____. 1990. "What do we mean by Law and Social Transformation?" *Canadian Journal of Law and Society* 5:1, 47–69.

Glavin, T. 1996a. *Dead Reckoning.* Vancouver: Greystone.

_____. 1996b and 1995. Interview notes.

_____. 1996c. "Shooting Fish in a Barrel." *Georgia Straight,* June 13, 13–18.

_____. 1996d. "Rebirth and the Volcano." *Georgia Straight,* May 2, 13–19.

_____. 1993. "The Fight for Fish." *Georgia Straight,* June 25, 7–12.

_____. 1987. "Laying claim to the future." *Vancouver Sun,* October 31, B1.

*Globe and Mail.* 1996. "Towards Native Justice." Editorial, February 17, A20.

_____. 1992. "A question of belonging." Editorial, April 2, A13.

_____. 1988a. "The Aboriginal future." Editorial, August 27, D2.

_____. 1988b. "Power in the reserves." Editorial, June 11, D6.

Grany, Wendy. 1991. "Where is our share?" *Vancouver Sun,* June 20, A17.

Griezic, F. 1996. "The Nisga'a agreement: a great deal or a great steal?" *Globe and Mail,*

May 5, A19.

Griffiths, C.T., et al. 1987. "Canadian Natives: Victims of Socio-Cultural Deprivation." *Human Organization* 46:3, 277–82.

Griffiths, C.T., and S.N. Verdun-Jones. 1989. *Canadian Criminal Justice.* Vancouver: Butterworths.

Hall, Tony. 1989a. "Warriors forgotten on Remembrance Day." *Globe and Mail,* November 10, A7.

_____ . 1989b. "As long as the sun shines." *Globe and Mail,* July 25, A7.

_____ . 1988. "Native Peoples: A search for dignity." *Globe and Mail,* August 2, A7.

Harding, Jim. 1991. "Policing and Aboriginal Justice." *Canadian Journal of Criminology* 33:3–4, 363–84.

Havemann, P. 1989. "Law, State, and Canada's Indigenous Peoples." In Caputo et al. (eds.), *Law, State and Society.* Toronto: Harcourt Brace Jovanovich.

Hay, D. 1975. *Albion's Fatal Tree.* London, U.K.: Penguin.

Hogben, D. 1994. "Ottawa laundering fish sales, panel hears." *Vancouver Sun,* November 30, A2.

Howard, R. 1996. "Endangered Species." *Globe and Mail,* July 20, D3.

Hume, M. 1996a. "DFO hasn't changed despite fish criticism." *Vancouver Sun,* June 21, A1.

_____ . 1996b. "Two fisheries experts support Nisga'a deal." *Vancouver Sun,* February 6, C1.

_____ . 1991. "We have minority rights for some, but not for others." *Vancouver Sun,* March 18, A12.

_____ . 1988. "Lost and Bitter Generation." *Vancouver Sun,* February 1, B1.

Hunter, M. 1995. Interview notes. President, Fisheries Council of B.C., Vancouver, B.C.

_____ . 1990. Letter to Bernard Valcourt, Minister of Fisheries and Oceans, June 12.

Hutchinson, A.C. 1992. "Still mostly middle-aged, rich, Christian, white men." *Globe and Mail,* Dercember 3, A19.

Isaac, T. 1993. "The power of constitutional language: the case against using 'aboriginal peoples' as a referent for First Nations." *Queen's Law Journal* 19, 415–42.

_____ . 1992a. "Discarding the Rose-Coloured Glasses: A Commentary on Asch and MacKlem." *Alberta Law Review* 30:2, 708–12.

_____ . 1992b. "The Nunavut Agreement-in-Principle and section 35 of the Constitution Act, 1982." *Manitoba Law Journal* 21, 390–405.

_____ . 1991. "Understanding the Sparrow Decision." *Queen's Law Journal* 16:2, 377–79.

Jackson, M.A., and C.T. Griffiths. 1991. *Canadian Criminology.* Toronto: Harcourt Brace Jovanovich.

Johnson, Eric. 1996. Personal communication. May 16.

Koss, P. 1991. "The Determination of Contractual Arrangements in the B.C. Market for Raw Fish." Unpublished paper prepared for the Department of Fisheries and Oceans, Vancouver, B.C.

Kulchyski, P. 1994. *Unjust Relations: Aboriginal Rights in Canadian Courts.* Toronto: Oxford University Press.

LaPierre, Carol. 1990. "The Role of Sentencing in the over-representation of Aboriginal People in Correctional Institutions." *Canadian Journal of Criminology* 32:3, 429–40.

# References

Lloyd, D., and M. Freeman. 1985. *Lloyd's Introduction to Jurisprudence.* Toronto: Carswell.

Lyon, N. 1992. "A perspective on the application of the Criminal Code to aboriginal peoples in light of R. v. Sparrow." *University of British Columbia Law Review,* 306–12.

MacQueen, K. 1991. "A Landmark ruling shocks anthropologists." *Vancouver Sun,* July 13, B2.

Mahoney, K.A. 1992. "The Constitutional Law of Equality in Canada." *Maine Law Review* 44:2, 229–60.

Makin, K. 1987. "Official cites bias in jailing of natives." *Globe and Mail,* September 29, A2.

Mandel, Michael. 1996. "The Dialectics of Constitutional Repression." In T. O'Reilly-Fleming (ed.), *Post-Critical Criminology.* Ontario: Prentice-Hall.

———. 1994. *The Charter of Rights and the Legalization of Politics in Canada.* 2nd ed. Toronto: Wall and Thompson.

———. 1989. *The Charter of Rights and the Legalization of Politics in Canada.* Toronto: Wall and Thompson.

Mandell, Louise. 1995. "The Birth of the White Buffalo." Unpublished paper.

Manitoba. 1991. *Public Inquiry into the Administration of Justice and Aboriginal Peoples.* Winnipeg: Queen's Printer.

Marchak, P. 1987. "Uncommon Property." In P. Marhak et al. (eds.), *Uncommon Property.* Toronto: Methuen.

Martin, R. 1991. "The Judges and the Charter." In S. Brickley and E. Comack (eds.), *The Social Basis of Law.* Toronto: Garamond.

Mason, G. 1987. "Tough, eloquent native leader." *Vancouver Sun,* March 28, A13.

Matas, R. 1993. "Leadership race seen as threat to B.C. Land talks." *Globe and Mail,* June 7, A4.

———. 1991. "When Worlds Collide." *Globe and Mail,* March 16.

McCormick, P. 1993. "Party Capability Theory and Appellate Success in the Supreme Court of Canada, 1949–1992." *Canadian Journal of Political Science* 26:3, 523–40.

McLintock, B. 1996. "Report warns of Mifflin aftermath." *Vancouver Province,* July 12, A2.

McNeil, K. 1993. "Envisaging Constitutional Space for Aboriginal Government." *Queen's Law Journal* 19, 95–136.

Mearns, J. 1995. Letter to the editor. *Vancouver Province,* August 17.

Menzies, C. 1996. Interview notes. Professor of Sociology, Department of Anthropology and Sociology, University of British Columbia, Vancouver, B.C.

Mickleburgh, R. 1993. "High Mortality Rates for Natives Confirmed." *Globe and Mail,* December 30, A6.

Millerd, D., and J. Nicol. 1994. *Report of the Fish Processing Strategic Task Force.* Victoria: Ministry of Agriculture, Fisheries and Food.

Milovanovic, D. 1988. *A Primer in the Sociology of Law.* U.S.: Harrow and Heston.

Moon, P. 1991. "Court struggles in chaos to combine law with compassion." *Globe and Mail,* March 4, A1.

Muszynski, A. 1987. "Shoreworkers and the UFAWU Organization." In P. Marchak et al. (eds.), *Uncommon Property.* Toronto: Methuen.

Newell, D. 1993. *Tangled Webs of History.* Toronto: University of Toronto Press.

Noble, I. 1996. "Treaties tabled at lunch." *North Shore News,* April 24, 3.

Nova Scotia. 1989. *The Royal Commission on the Donald Marshall Jr., Prosecution.* Halifax.

Nutt, R. 1996. "Court rejects bid to block Houston mine." *Vancouver Sun,* July 12, D1.

O'Neil, P. 1996a. "Exploitation of 'Indian lands' assailed." *Vancouver Sun,* July 11, A1.

_____. 1996b. "B.C. wants more control over fish." *Vancouver Sun,* June 17, A1.

_____. 1991. "Campbell dismisses fear of biased Hearing." *Vancouver Sun,* March 28, A9.

Ontario Federation of Anglers and Hunters. 1994. "Problems Arising from *Sparrow."* September.Toronto: Ontario Federation of Anglers and Hunters.

Pearse, P. 1982. *Turning the Tide: A New Policy for Canada's Pacific Fisheries.* Commission on Pacific Fisheries Policy, final report, September. Cat. no. Fs 23-18/ 1982E. Ottawa: Supply and Services Canada.

Pennier, C. 1995. "Legal Lessons." *Vancouver Province,* September 10, A34.

Picard, A. 1991. "The Internal Exiles of Canada." *Globe and Mail*, September 7, D3.

_____. 1990. "75-Day Mohawk seige has longer precedents." *Globe and Mail,* September 24, A5.

Pinkerton, E. 1987. "Competition Among B.C. Fish-Processing Firms." In P. Marchak et al. (eds.), *Uncommon Property.* Toronto: Methuen.

Platiel, R. 1995. "Natives 'criminalized' unfairly, critics charge." *Globe and Mail,* October 17, A7.

_____. 1993. "Churches say native rights still abused by government." *Globe and Mail,* June 4, A3.

_____. 1992. "Fighting for Home and Native Land." *Globe and Mail,* March 2, A1.

_____. 1991a. "Suicide increase troubles natives." *Globe and Mail,* June 3, A1.

_____. 1991b. "The Third Solitude." *Globe and Mail,* April 13, D1.

_____. 1990. "Aboriginal Justice System recommended." *Globe and Mail,* August 3, D1.

_____. 1988a. "Young Inuit facing a future of welfare, crime, study says." *Globe and Mail,* August 24, A1.

_____. 1988b. "Cold starts in the morning." *Globe and Mail,* February 2, A13.

_____. 1987. "Natives perform special ceremonies to honour war dead." *Globe and Mail,* November 12, A5.

Point, Steven. 1996. Personal communication.

Ponting, J.R., ed. 1986. *Arduous Journey.* Toronto: McClelland and Stewart.

Price Waterhouse. 1989. *The Fishing Industry in British Columbia.* A report prepared for the Fisheries Council of B.C. Vancouver.

Ratner, R.S. 1991. "Critical Criminology: A splendid oxymoron." *Journal of Human Justice* 1:1, 3–9.

Roberts, D. 1992a. "Separate Native justice rejected for Manitoba." *Globe and Mail,* January 30, A1.

_____. 1992b. "Parallel panel hears native inmates." *Globe and Mail,* January 30, A4.

Roberts, D., and G. York. 1991. "Judges Urge Separate Native Justice System." *Globe and Mail,* August 30, A1.

Ryder, B. 1994. "Aboriginal Rights and Delamuukw v. The Queen." *Constitutional Forum* 5, 43–48.

Sanders, D. 1990. "The Supreme Court of Canada and the 'Legal and Political Struggle' over Indigenous Rights." *Canadian Ethnic Studies* 22:3, 124–31.

# References

_____. 1989. "Pre-Existing Rights: Aboriginal Peoples of Canada." In G. Beaudoin and E. Ratushny (eds.), *The Canadian Charter of Rights and Freedoms*. 2nd ed. Vancouver: Carswell.

Sargent, N.C. 1991. "Rethinking the Law and Social Transformation." *Journal of Human Justice* 3:1, 1–6.

Schwartz, B. 1992. "Law and Society." *Globe and Mail,* August, A18.

Schwindt, R. 1996. "The case for an expanded Indian salmon fishing." *Market Solutions for Native Poverty.* Vancouver: C.D. Howe Institute.

Sheppard, R. 1992. "Native Justice: Let's take the plunge." *Globe and Mail,* January 30, A17.

Simpson, J. 1996. "When it comes to fish, provinces should be aware of what they demand." *Globe and Mail,* June 19, A24.

_____. 1995a. "Letter to Captain Canada." *Globe and Mail,* April 25, A18.

_____. 1995b. "A lot of hypocritical breast-beating about conservation of fish." *Globe and Mail,* March 21, A18.

Simpson, S. 1993. "Natives vow never to quit legal fight for land claims." *Vancouver Sun,* June 18, A9.

Slattery, B. 1992. "First Nations and the Constitution: A Question of Trust." *Canadian Bar Review* 71, 261–93.

_____. 1983. "The Constitutional Guarantees of Aboriginal and Treaty Rights." *Queen's Law Journal* 8, 232–73.

Smith, C. 1996. "Fraser River natives claim betrayal by feds on fishery." *Georgia Straight,* August 8, 7.

Smith, J. 1995. "Natives take salmon battle to court." *Vancouver Province,* August 17, A5.

Smith, M. 1995. *Our Home or Native Land.* Victoria: Crown Western.

Southam News. 1992. "Ex-Justice pleads for cut program." *Vancouver Sun*, March 18, A12.

Spicer, K. 1991. *Citizen's Forum on Canada's Future.* Ottawa.

Tennant, C. 1991. "Justification and Cultural Authority in s. 35(1) of the Constitution Act, 1982." *Dalhousie Law Journal* 14:2, 372–86.

Thatcher, R.W. 1986. "The Functions of Minority Group Disrepute." In B. MacLean, (ed.), *The Political Economy of Crime.* Toronto: Prentice-Hall.

Thompson, E.P. 1977. *Whigs and Hunters: The Origins of the Black Act.* Harmondsworth: Penguin.

Todd, J. 1988. "A people loses its way of life." *Vancouver Sun,* February 13, B2.

Turpel, M.F. 1989. "Aboriginal Peoples and the Canadian Charter of Rights and Freedoms." *Canadian Human Rights Yearbook* 6:3, 3–43.

University of Victoria. 1990. Papers from "The Sparrow Case" conference, November 19. Victoria, B.C.

Valentine, V.F. 1980. "Native Peoples and Canadian Society." In R. Breton et al. (eds.), *Cultural Boundaries and the Cohesion of Canada.* Montreal: Institute for Research on Public Policy.

Valpy, M. 1996. "Bullying the Chippewas over fish." *Globe and Mail,* July 9, A17.

_____. 1993. "The Destruction of the Labrador Innui." *Globe and Mail,* February 5, A2.

*Vancouver Sun.* 1995. "Indians mishandled funds." November 23, A1

_____. 1987. "No big solution on native rights." Editorial, March 28, A13.

Weber, M. 1978. *Economy and Society, Vols I & II.* Ed. Guenther Roth and Claus

2

22

Wittich. University of California Press.

Weinfeld, M. 1989. "Canada's Racism Record." *Globe and Mail,* July 18, A7.

Williamson, R. 1996. "Disaster lurks in salmon fishing proposals." *Globe and Mail,* February 8, B7.

Wilson, D. 1993. "Indians old struggle goes space-age." *Globe and Mail*, June 7, A4.

Wright, R. 1992a. *Stolen Continents.* Toronto: Houghton-Mifflin.

_____ . 1992b. "Let's not make a deal without the natives." *Globe and Mail,* August 11, A15.

York, G. 1991. "Justice report stirs caution." *Globe and Mail,* August 31, A1.

_____ . 1989. *The Dispossessed.* Toronto: Lester and Orpen Dennys.